COUNTRY FAIR
COOKBOOK

Other cookbooks by FARM JOURNAL

FARM JOURNAL'S COUNTRY COOKBOOK

FREEZING & CANNING COOKBOOK

FARM JOURNAL'S COMPLETE PIE COOKBOOK

LET'S START TO COOK

HOMEMADE BREAD

AMERICA'S BEST VEGETABLE RECIPES

HOMEMADE CANDY

BUSY WOMAN'S COOKBOOK

HOMEMADE COOKIES

HOMEMADE ICE CREAM AND CAKE

INFORMAL ENTERTAINING COUNTRY STYLE

FAMILY FAVORITES FROM COUNTRY KITCHENS

EVERYDAY COOKING WITH HERBS

THE THRIFTY COOK

BY THE FOOD EDITORS OF *FARM JOURNAL*

COUNTRY FAIR COOKBOOK

Every Recipe a Blue Ribbon Winner

Edited by ELISE W. MANNING
FARM JOURNAL Food Editor

Photography Supervised by AL J. REAGAN

Doubleday & Company, Inc.
Garden City, New York

Library of Congress Cataloging in Publication Data

Main entry under title:
Country fair cookbook.

    Includes index.
    1. Cookery, American.   I. Manning, Elise W., ed.
II. Title.
TX715.C8614   641.5
ISBN 0-385-02249-2
Library of Congress Catalog Card Number 74–12687

CONTENTS

COLOR ILLUSTRATIONS

Color photographs by: William Hazzard/Hazzard Studios and Ken Bronstein/
Mel Richman Studios

Introduction

HEIGH-HO!
COME TO THE FAIR

Every year from July to October, more than 70 million people walk through the main gate of the fairgrounds. Fairs are exciting events from New Hampshire to California. Band music reverberates as vendors display clusters of balloons and sell big puffs of cotton candy. The Ferris wheels are turning in the air and merry-go-round calliope music can be heard above the crowds. There are a staggering number of exhibits to see—from the fat calves groomed to the hoof to gee-whiz farm machinery and art shows.

One of the most popular spots is the building that houses exhibits of food specialties entered with hopes of a Blue Ribbon or at least a White Ribbon. Of course, if a winner comes home with the distinguished Purple Ribbon, which is awarded for an outstanding entry, that is the ultimate! Usually the Blue Ribbon is awarded for excellent quality, far above average; the Red Ribbon indicates an above-average entry; a White Ribbon, average quality. Standards vary from fair to fair, as we discovered when we visited food exhibits the country over. Some fairs are extremely tough and only the very finest entries get a chance at even a White Ribbon. But a White Ribbon at one fair might be a Blue Ribbon award at another fair where the judging is not so severe.

Farm women take an important part in the fair exhibits. Many have been planning all year exactly which of their prized recipes they will enter and hopefully win the coveted Blue Ribbon. There is usually a small cash award too, but that is not the important factor in competing in the fair—it's the challenge, satisfaction and pride in winning a Blue Ribbon.

We took a swing around the country to visit fairs and to talk with winners and judges. We came early and watched a fair grow as crews worked almost all night to set up exhibits, displays—even building kitchens for demonstrations.

"Entering fairs gets into your blood," a farm homemaker told us. "Every year I think I am too busy to bake and exhibit, but the pull is too strong and I decide to bake just a few loaves of bread. Next thing I know I have turned out 25 entries. I have won over 1,000 ribbons in the past 25 years."

Still another fine cook told us proudly that she comes home every year with several "Blues"; she has 300 ribbons displayed on her kitchen wall. A Grand Champion Winner in the Cake Division at the Kansas State Fair pointed out the Blue Ribbons she had won and said she had learned to bake under her father's stern eye. By the time she was eighteen, she was baking beautiful, high, tender-crumbed cakes for their family-owned bakery.

Getting ready for the fair is serious business and many women start baking two weeks ahead of entry day. Others bake and freeze several months ahead, while some have a three-day marathon of baking everything at the last minute.

Up bright and early one morning to watch the women bring in their entries, we found them starting to arrive by 7 o'clock, lugging well-tied boxes to the judges' table. They looked weary but excited and slightly apprehensive as they unpacked their treasures and retired to the background to observe the judging.

Most of the food judges are experienced home economists and take their responsibilities very seriously. At state fairs and at some local fairs, a discriminating eye and a keen sense of taste are "musts" in order to be a competent judge. At one fair we visited we discovered that the three women who were to decide upon the best of the show had accumulated 65 years of judging.

We watched a judge as she picked up a biscuit. Breaking it open, she studied the texture, checked the top surface for even browning, broke off a piece and chewed slowly and thought-fully, then reflected a few seconds before she made her decision. The biscuit was either placed to the left to be discarded or to the right for further consideration and a possible ribbon.

Before going on the next category she sucked a lemon and took a sip of water. Then she alternated sweets with non-sweets for change of pace. Finally after a careful study and perhaps a second taste or two, she would make her decision and point to first, second and third choices for the ribbons. Meanwhile one of the fair staff workers was busily slicing bread, cakes, pies, for the judges to taste. Another was arranging cookies and dough-nuts on paper plates and a third carefully wrote the winning entries into the record book.

After the judging, women will come up and ask why they placed only second or third—or not at all. The judges explain in detail and give them helpful pointers for next year.

"Some women do not plan their oven times wisely and at-tempt to bake too many foods in a day," judges say. This throws the temperature off and results in biscuits or cookies that are too brown on the bottom . . . or cakes with a tough crust, due to too high a baking temperature. It is important to organize the baking so that if possible you can bake everything that requires the same temperature the same day. Or if that is not possible then be sure to let the oven cool down or go up to the correct temperature, as the case may be. Some cooks try to do too much, resulting in quantity but the quality suffers and they miss out on a ribbon.

The day after judging, fair committee members are working nonstop as they place all the winners on clean paper plates or foil-covered cardboard. All glass cases are washed and shined until they are crystal clear. Then the winners in all divisions are placed neatly in their categories on the shelves with their respec-tive ribbons. By the end of the day (and that is often midnight) everything is in apple-pie order. The booths are assembled, every exhibit is finished, the workmen have packed up the last of their tools and everyone says a weary good night. The next day the fair opens . . . and as one tired fair worker said triumphantly, "Well, we made it through another year—it's a lot of work but it's worth it."

In this book we invite you to share with us the excitement and the pride and excellence we discovered at the fairs. We sifted through a big collection of Blue and Purple winners, read them all, and then started testing and perfecting the recipes in our FARM JOURNAL Countryside Test Kitchens. Each recipe was re-tested and in some cases slight adjustments were made until they came up to our standards and would be as "foolproof" as possible.

In this selection of prize-winning recipes from fairs all over the country you will find tall, beautiful cakes including some "show stoppers," decorated cakes for special events, crunchy cookies, velvet-crumbed breads, feather-light rolls, biscuits, doughnuts and a wonderful array of tender-crusted pies.

We think you will be proud to serve any of these winning recipes to your family and friends.

Chapter 1

HOMEMADE BREADS . . .
COUNTRY FAIR BOUNTY

On many a farm in late summer the alarm shrills loudly at 4:00 A.M.—the big day has arrived. It's time to start baking the prized yeast bread, cinnamon rolls and fruit-studded tea ring to take to the fair. And hopefully to win a Blue Ribbon.

By 10:00 A.M. weary, but happy women are carrying their carefully packed treasures into the "arts" building at the fair. There's a luscious smell of faintly warm breads and rolls as the members of the fair workers committee lift each entry from the box and line them up for the judges.

Fat, crusty loaves of rye bread, tender-crumbed white, sturdy whole wheat loaves browned to perfection, tea breads, golden-crumbed coffee cakes and tea rings gorgeous with red and green cherries and citron.

The women watch quietly as the judges study the crust, feel the crumb, nibble a sample and then finally make the big decision—a Blue Ribbon is placed alongside a particular tall, handsome loaf of white bread.

At the state fair in Utah we chatted with a happy winner —she not only won a Blue for her white bread but captured the Sweepstake Ribbon in the Baked Goods Division, and her daughter was awarded the Sweepstake Ribbon in Canning Division. "My ambition this year was to win a Blue on my white bread and finally after working for two years to perfect the recipe I reached my goal. I tell my children even if you lose, you haven't failed, for you always learn something—never be afraid to try. I've learned to experiment with a recipe until I am satisfied—no one can imagine the work and time involved getting ready to enter the competition at the fair—but we love it because it is such a challenge."

And a North Carolina winner says: "My love for making yeast breads started when I was a young girl. There were nine in our family and my mother never stopped baking, it seemed. She would let me 'work down' the yeast dough. I loved the silky feeling of the dough, the aroma and the taste of a thick slice of bread still warm and fragrant from the oven. Since then I have made a 'mountain' of homemade breads for my own family. I won a Blue Ribbon at the agricultural fair for my Golden Whole Wheat Loaves—do try them," she urged.

Still another top winner from Wisconsin explained her feelings about competing at the fair. "Fair time in our family is a busy, happy and exciting time. Both my mother and mother-in-law are excellent cooks and we all enter breads and cakes at our fair. As the judge samples my cake she'll say 'this is good'; then she tastes my mother's cake and states 'this is better.' Next she nibbles my mother-in-law's entry and says 'this is the best.' I get third prize again. But when my Graham Muffins came up for judging—I came home with the Blue Ribbon."

An outstanding cook and multi-ribbon winner told us: "I won my first Purple Ribbon at the Iowa State Fair and my family just beamed with pride. First, I won the Quick Bread Division in Cass County. Then my entry was sent to the state contest where all 99 counties of Iowa were competing. Out of these 99 entries, five quick breads are selected to be demonstrated at the state fair. My recipe was one of the five and I won first place." We asked where she got her recipe. "It's my original," she said. "I experimented until I came up with just the right combination of flavor and texture. I love to cook for my farmer husband and two youngsters. They always praise my Onion Cheese Bread and the barbecued ribs I serve with it."

We have tested dozens of the very best breads, rolls, quick breads, biscuits, muffins and doughnuts—winners at the fairs, and we think you will be successful with all of them.

How to Judge Perfect Yeast Bread

An excellent loaf of yeast bread should have an evenly rounded top and be symmetrical in size and with no cracks, bulges or bumps. Between the sides and top, there should be a "break," which should be even and have a well-shredded look. Crusts on all yeast breads should be crisp and tender. The interior color should be uniform with no light or dark streaks and should feel soft and fine with no crumbliness. The crumb should have many small even holes.

Breads made from batters will have less uniform holes and will be more open in grain than those made from doughs. The crumb of batter bread should be tender and moist and tear easily with uniform texture. There should be a sweet nutty fragrance and flavor even after bread is cold.

Breads, sweet breads and rolls that contain chopped fruits or nuts should show an even distribution of the fruit or nuts and their flavor should not overpower the bread. Rolls should be evenly plump and hold their shape. Sweet breads should be symmetrical in design and not over-iced or overdecorated.

COMMON PROBLEMS WITH YEAST BREADS . . . AND PROBABLE CAUSES

Cracks, bulges or bumps—not kneaded properly, too much dough in pan, cooled too quickly or too long a rising period.

Poor volume—yeast killed by too high a temperature, not enough flour or short rising period.

No shred or "break"—not kneaded enough or wrong type of flour.

Large air cells—too long rising period in pan, too cool an oven, not enough flour or insufficient kneading.

Heavy, close, compact cells—yeast killed by too high a temperature, poor distribution of ingredients or too cool when rising.

Heavy, dry, crumbly crumb—wrong type of flour, too stiff a dough (too much flour), too cool an oven or insufficient kneading.

Gray or streaked crumb—wrong type of flour (all-purpose flour should be used), poorly mixed or too much flour added while shaping the loaf, improper length of rising periods.

Sour flavor—too long a rising period or inferior ingredients.

Yeasty flavor—too long a rising period or high temperature in the kitchen.

Tough crust—insufficient proofing (not doubled in bulk) or too much handling of risen dough.

Pale crust—too low a baking temperature, too much salt, drying of dough during rising or too little sugar.

Crackled crust—too rapid cooling in a draft.

TIPS TO HELP YOU BAKE A PERFECT LOAF OF BREAD

Be sure that the yeast is fresh. Check date on the packet of active dry yeast; if the expiration date has passed, do not risk using it. Compressed yeast when fresh should be gray-white and should crumble easily.

Use good-quality flour. Use flour labeled "all-purpose" or "bread flour."

Use good-quality fresh shortening. Shortening aids in the proper development of the dough, enabling the gluten to stretch and retain the gas. It helps to produce a tender crumb, maintain freshness and improves the eating quality of the bread.

Be sure to mix and knead dough thoroughly. Many cooks prefer to mix in the last half of the flour with their hands because they can squeeze the dough between the fingers. The sides of the bowl should be cleaned as the flour is added. If the dough seems sticky after it is out on the board, add flour just a little at a time as you knead. Knead until little bubbles can be seen beneath the surface of the dough.

Old flour can produce an inferior loaf of bread. If the flour has been carried over a hot summer or if it was purchased at a store with low turnover, it will produce poor bread. It may actually smell rancid or musty and should be thrown away. The gluten in old flour has deteriorated and cannot produce the elastic yeast dough that it should.

Always preheat the oven at least 10 to 15 minutes before bread is ready to bake. If the oven is not up to the proper temperature, the dough will continue to slowly rise and could collapse.

If bread dough seems hard to handle during the kneading and does not feel elastic as it should, pick up the dough and throw it down on the counter to make it easier to handle and knead.

Flour tends to dry out during the winter months. You might find that your recipe does not need as much flour as it did in the summer months. Mix and knead as usual but keep the dough slightly on the soft side and the results will be a light bread with a silky texture.

Never add chilled ingredients, such as fruits or nuts that have been stored in the refrigerator, to a dough as they will slow down the rising. Warm the chilled ingredients in a piece of aluminum foil in a very slow oven for just a few minutes.

Breads that are made with milk will take a little longer to bake than those made with water because of the milk protein and milk solids. It may be necessary to cover the loaves with brown paper the last half of the baking period so that the top surface will not become too dark before the interior of the bread is done.

How to Judge Perfect Baking Powder Biscuits

An excellent baking powder biscuit should be light, tender, high and golden brown with a smooth level top. The biscuits when pulled apart should be flaky and slightly moist.

COMMON PROBLEMS WITH BAKING POWDER BISCUITS . . . AND PROBABLE CAUSES

Low volume—too little leavening, overmixing, excess shortening or oven temperature too high.

Dark bottom crust—baked on darkened baking sheet.

Yellow or brown spots—excess leavening or undermixing.

Excess flour on crust—too much flour sprinkled on pastry cloth.

Toughness—too little shortening, too much liquid or flour or overmixing.

Not flaky—too little shortening, too much mixing or too little kneading.

Coarse uneven cells—too much leavening or undermixing.

Dry—too much flour or too long baking.

TIPS TO HELP YOU BAKE A PERFECT BISCUIT

Cut the shortening into dry ingredients with a pastry blender until mixture looks like fine crumbs.

Knead the dough 15 to 20 times, turning dough after each kneading. This combines ingredients thoroughly to make light, fluffy biscuits.

Cut rolled biscuit dough with a cutter that has been dipped in flour, then tap sharply to remove excess flour. Cut biscuit with a firm downward pressure.

Do not twist the cutter as it will distort the shape of the biscuit.

For biscuits with crusty sides, place them about 1 inch apart on ungreased baking sheet. For soft-sided biscuits, arrange them close together in an ungreased pan.

How to Judge Perfect Muffins

An excellent muffin should be light, in fact so light that when a muffin is picked up in the hand, you are amazed that it weighs so little.

The outside should be golden brown, symmetrical in shape, with no tendency to form a peak or knob at the top. The top surface should be slightly pebbled, rather than smooth and even.

The interior of the muffin should have round fairly uniformly sized holes with no long slender tunnels.

COMMON PROBLEMS WITH MUFFINS . . . AND PROBABLE CAUSES

Peaked, smooth crust—overmixed.
Pale—temperature too low or overmixed.
Dry and crumbly—excess flour, oven temperature too low or overbaking.
Tunnels—overmixing.
Toughness—overmixing.

TIPS TO HELP YOU BAKE A PERFECT MUFFIN

Mix liquid and flour mixture only until flour is moistened; the batter will look lumpy. Do not overmix.

Fill each muffin cup ⅔ full with batter.

Remove muffins with a spatula from pans immediately to prevent their steaming and becoming soggy.

COUNTRY YEAST AND BATTER BREADS

The fairs' finest are represented in this bevy of golden-crusted loaves of white bread we share with you—each one fine-grained, well shaped with the sweet nutty flavor of homemade. One from a Missouri fair winner has earned five Blue Ribbons. Another winner from a Wisconsin fair tells us that her grandmother taught her the fine art of making a beautiful loaf of bread and she wins every time with her White Yeast Loaf.

You'll want to cut thick slices of the Honey Whole Wheat, a high sturdy loaf with full-bodied flavor that won a Blue Ribbon in Oklahoma. And the Molasses Rye not only won a Blue Ribbon at a Kansas fair but is now sold at a shop because so many people wanted her bread.

Rich, nourishing High-Protein Bread made with cottage cheese and buttermilk was a first-time winner at the Oklahoma fair. Everyone loved the Oatmeal Bread winner at the Ohio fair: honey gives it a sweet flavor and poppy seeds, a special look.

There are many quick and easy batter breads—Cottage Cheese Dill, plump loaves with light texture and good flavor. Fat sturdy loaves of Herbed Batter Bread, a winner at a Nebraska fair, have a delightful mingling of sage, caraway seeds and nutmeg. Still another Blue from Nebraska is Rye Batter Bread, made from rye flour, honey and caraway seeds. "This is a favorite at our house—you have to taste it to appreciate the good country flavor," this excellent bread maker told us.

GENEVIEVE'S WHITE BREAD

This woman is well known in Utah for her bread

2½ c. milk, scalded
3 tblsp. shortening
3 tblsp. sugar
1 tblsp. salt

1 pkg. active dry yeast
¼ c. lukewarm water
7 c. sifted flour

Combine milk, shortening, sugar and salt. Cool to lukewarm.

Sprinkle yeast on lukewarm water; stir to dissolve. Add yeast and 4 c. flour to milk mixture. Beat with electric mixer at medium speed until smooth, about 2 minutes, scraping bowl occasionally. Or beat with spoon until batter is smooth. Cover and let rise 45 minutes.

Gradually stir in 2 c. flour, mixing to make a soft dough. Turn out on floured surface, using remaining 1 c. flour as needed to keep dough from sticking. Knead dough until smooth and satiny, about 15 minutes.

Place dough in lightly greased bowl; turn over to grease top. Cover and let rise in warm place 20 minutes.

Knead dough down in bowl for 2 minutes. Turn over and let rise 20 minutes. Repeat kneading and rising once more.

Turn dough out on floured surface. Let rest 10 minutes. Divide dough in half. Shape each half into a loaf and place in 2 greased 8½×4½×2½" loaf pans. Let rise until doubled, about 45 minutes.

Bake in 350° oven 50 minutes or until loaves sound hollow when tapped. Remove from pans; cool on racks. Makes 2.

DELICIOUS WHITE BREAD

This easy-to-mix white bread takes less time to rise

2 pkgs. active dry yeast	1 tblsp. salt
2¾ c. lukewarm water	⅓ c. cooking oil
½ c. nonfat dry milk	7 to 7½ c. sifted flour
2 tblsp. sugar	

Sprinkle yeast on lukewarm water; stir to dissolve. Add dry milk, sugar, salt, oil and 3 c. flour. Beat with electric mixer at medium speed until smooth, about 3 minutes, scraping bowl occasionally. Or beat with spoon until batter is smooth.

Gradually add enough remaining flour to make a soft dough that leaves the sides of the bowl. Cover; let rest 15 minutes.

Knead on floured surface until smooth and satiny, about 5 minutes. Divide dough in half. Shape each half into a loaf and place in 2 greased 9×5×3" loaf pans. Let rise until doubled, about 1 to 1½ hours.

Bake in 400° oven 30 to 35 minutes or until loaves sound hollow when tapped. Remove from pans; cool on racks. Makes 2 loaves.

PERFECT WHITE BREAD

Spread thick slices of this crusty bread with jam

2 c. milk, scalded	1 pkg. active dry yeast
1 tblsp. shortening	¼ c. lukewarm water
2 tblsp. sugar	5¾ to 6¼ c. sifted flour
2 tsp. salt	

Combine milk, shortening, sugar and salt. Cool to lukewarm.

Sprinkle yeast on lukewarm water; stir to dissolve. Add yeast and 2 c. flour to milk mixture. Beat with electric mixer at medium speed until smooth, about 2 minutes, scraping bowl occasionally. Or beat with spoon until batter is smooth.

Gradually add enough remaining flour to make a soft dough

that leaves the sides of the bowl. Turn out on floured surface and knead until smooth and satiny, about 10 minutes.

Place dough in lightly greased bowl; turn over to grease top. Cover and let rise in warm place until doubled, about 1 to 1½ hours.

Punch down. Divide dough in half. Shape each half into a loaf and place in 2 greased 8½×4½×2½″ loaf pans. Let rise until doubled, about 45 minutes.

Bake in 400° oven 35 minutes or until loaves sound hollow when tapped. Remove from pans; cool on racks. Makes 2 loaves.

BLUE RIBBON WHITE BREAD

An Oklahoma homemaker shares her bread recipe with us

2¼ c. hot water
1 c. nonfat dry milk
3 tblsp. shortening
2 tblsp. sugar
2 tsp. salt
1 pkg. active dry yeast

¼ c. lukewarm water
¼ tsp. ground ginger
6 c. sifted flour
1 egg white, slightly beaten
1 tblsp. water

Combine 2¼ c. hot water, dry milk, shortening, sugar and salt. Cool to lukewarm.

Sprinkle yeast on ¼ c. lukewarm water; stir to dissolve. Add yeast, ginger and 2 c. flour to milk mixture. Beat with electric mixer at medium speed until smooth, about 2 minutes, scraping bowl occasionally. Or beat with spoon until batter is smooth.

Gradually add enough remaining flour to make a soft dough that leaves the sides of the bowl. Turn out on floured surface and knead until smooth and satiny, about 8 to 10 minutes.

Place dough in lightly greased bowl; turn over to grease top. Cover and let rise in warm place until doubled, about 1 to 1½ hours.

Punch down. Let rise again until doubled, about 45 minutes.

Divide dough in half. Shape each half into a loaf and place in 2 greased 8½×4½×2½″ loaf pans. Brush with combined egg white and 1 tblsp. water. Let rise until doubled, about 45 minutes.

Bake in 400° oven 25 minutes or until loaves sound hollow when tapped. Remove from pans; cool on racks. Makes 2 loaves.

PRIZE-WINNING WHITE BREAD

High, elegant yeast loaves that will please your family

3¾ c. lukewarm milk	1½ tblsp. salt
3½ tblsp. shortening	2 pkgs. active dry yeast
4½ tblsp. sugar	8½ c. sifted flour

Combine milk, shortening, sugar and salt.

Combine yeast with 4½ c. flour. Add to milk mixture. Beat with electric mixer at medium speed until smooth, about 2 minutes, scraping bowl occasionally. Or beat with spoon until batter is smooth.

Gradually add enough remaining flour to make a soft dough that leaves the sides of the bowl. Turn out on floured surface and knead until smooth and satiny, about 8 to 10 minutes.

Place dough in lightly greased bowl; turn over to grease top. Cover and let rise in warm place until doubled, about 1½ to 2 hours.

Punch down. Let rise again until doubled, about 45 minutes.

Divide dough in half. Shape each half into a loaf and place in 2 greased 9×5×3" loaf pans. Let rise until doubled, about 45 minutes.

Bake in 400° oven 35 minutes or until loaves sound hollow when tapped. Remove from pans; cool on racks. Makes 2 loaves.

WHITE YEAST LOAVES

A home economics student won a ribbon for this bread

1½ c. milk, scalded	2 pkgs. active dry yeast
½ c. shortening	½ c. lukewarm water
½ c. sugar	2 eggs
2 tsp. salt	7 to 7½ c. sifted flour

Combine milk, shortening, sugar and salt. Cool to lukewarm.

Sprinkle yeast on lukewarm water; stir to dissolve. Add yeast, eggs and 2 c. flour to milk mixture. Beat with electric mixer at medium speed until smooth, about 2 minutes, scraping bowl occasionally. Or beat with spoon until batter is smooth.

Gradually add enough remaining flour to make a soft dough that leaves the sides of the bowl. Turn out on floured surface and knead until smooth and satiny, about 5 minutes.

Place dough in lightly greased bowl; turn over to grease top. Cover and let rise in warm place until doubled, about 1½ hours.

Punch down. Let rise again until doubled, about 45 minutes.

Divide dough in half. Shape each half into a loaf and place in 2 greased 9×5×3" loaf pans. Let rise again until doubled, about 45 minutes.

Bake in 375° oven 35 minutes or until loaves sound hollow when tapped. Remove from pans; cool on racks. Makes 2 loaves.

GOLDEN SESAME BRAID

Slice and place in a long napkin-lined basket for dinner

1½ c. milk, scalded	3 eggs
¼ c. shortening	7½ c. sifted flour
¼ c. sugar	1 egg, beaten
1 tblsp. salt	1 tblsp. water
1 pkg. active dry yeast	2 tblsp. sesame seeds
½ c. lukewarm water	

Combine milk, shortening, sugar and salt. Cool to lukewarm.

Sprinkle yeast on lukewarm water; stir to dissolve. Add yeast, 3 eggs and 2 c. flour to milk mixture. Beat with electric mixer at medium speed until smooth, about 2 minutes, scraping bowl occasionally. Or beat with spoon until batter is smooth.

Gradually add enough remaining flour to make a soft dough that leaves the sides of the bowl. Turn out on floured surface and knead until smooth and satiny, about 8 to 10 minutes.

Place dough in lightly greased bowl; turn over to grease top. Cover and let rise in warm place until doubled, about 1 hour.

Divide dough into 6 parts. Roll each into a 12" strip. Braid

3 strips together to form loaf and place on 2 greased baking sheets. Cover and let rise until doubled, about 45 minutes.

Brush braids with a glaze using 1 beaten egg and 1 tblsp. water. Sprinkle with sesame seeds.

Bake in 350° oven 30 minutes or until loaves sound hollow when tapped. Remove from baking sheets; cool on racks. Makes 2 loaves.

HONEY WHOLE WHEAT LOAVES

Makes good breakfast toast and so nutritious, too

1 c. milk	2 pkgs. active dry yeast
¼ c. butter or regular margarine	1½ c. lukewarm water
	2½ c. sifted flour
2 tblsp. sugar	5 c. whole wheat flour
½ c. honey	2 tblsp. melted butter or
1 tblsp. salt	regular margarine

Scald milk. Stir in ¼ c. butter, sugar, honey and salt. Cool to lukewarm.

Sprinkle yeast on lukewarm water; stir to dissolve. Add yeast, flour and 2½ c. whole wheat flour to milk mixture. Beat with electric mixer at medium speed until smooth, about 2 minutes, scraping bowl occasionally. Or beat with spoon until batter is smooth.

Gradually add enough whole wheat flour to make a soft dough that leaves the sides of the bowl. Turn out on floured surface. Let rest 10 minutes.

Knead dough until smooth and satiny, about 10 minutes. Place dough in lightly greased bowl; turn over to grease top. Cover and let rise in warm place until doubled, about 1½ hours.

Divide dough in half. Shape each half into a loaf and place in 2 greased 9×5×3" loaf pans. Let rise until doubled, about 45 minutes.

Bake in 400° oven 40 to 50 minutes or until loaves sound hollow when tapped. Remove from pans; cool on racks. Makes 2 loaves.

REFRIGERATED WHOLE WHEAT BREAD

Prepare the loaves ahead; pop into the oven the next day

1¾ c. milk	2 pkgs. active dry yeast
3 tblsp. butter or regular	½ c. lukewarm water
margarine	4 c. sifted flour
⅓ c. honey	2 c. whole wheat flour
1 tblsp. salt	

Scald milk. Stir in butter, honey and salt. Cool to lukewarm.

Sprinkle yeast on lukewarm water; stir to dissolve. Add yeast, 1 c. flour and whole wheat flour to milk mixture. Beat with electric mixer at medium speed until smooth, about 2 minutes, scraping bowl occasionally.

Gradually add enough remaining flour to make a soft dough that leaves the sides of the bowl. Turn out on floured surface and knead until smooth and no longer sticky, about 8 minutes. Cover and let rest 20 minutes.

Divide dough in half. Shape each half into a loaf and place in 2 greased 8½ ×4½ ×2½ ″ loaf pans. Cover pans loosely with greased waxed paper and then cover with plastic wrap. Refrigerate 22 to 24 hours.

When ready to bake, remove from refrigerator and uncover. Let stand 10 minutes at room temperature.

Bake in 400° oven 35 to 40 minutes or until loaves sound hollow when tapped. Remove from pans; cool on racks. Makes 2.

GOLDEN WHOLE WHEAT LOAVES

The woman who sent in this recipe loves to bake yeast bread

1 pkg. active dry yeast	½ c. brown sugar, firmly
1½ c. lukewarm water	packed
2 c. sifted flour	3 tblsp. shortening
2 tblsp. sugar	3½ c. whole wheat flour
1 tblsp. salt	Melted butter or regular
½ c. hot water	margarine

Sprinkle yeast on 1½ c. lukewarm water; stir to dissolve. Add flour, sugar and salt. Beat with electric mixer at medium speed until smooth, about 2 minutes, scraping bowl occasionally. Or beat with spoon until batter is smooth. Cover and let rise in warm place until light and bubbly.

Combine ½ c. hot water, brown sugar and shortening. Cool to lukewarm.

Add brown sugar mixture to yeast; mix well. Gradually add enough whole wheat flour to make a soft dough that leaves the sides of the bowl. Turn out on floured surface and knead until smooth and satiny, about 10 minutes.

Place dough in lightly greased bowl; turn over to grease top. Cover and let rise until doubled, about 1½ hours.

Divide dough in half. Shape into balls; let rest 15 minutes. Shape each half into a loaf and place in 2 greased 9×5×3" loaf pans. Let rise until doubled, about 45 minutes.

Bake in 350° oven 40 minutes or until loaves sound hollow when tapped. Remove from pans; cool on racks. While still hot, brush tops of loaves with melted butter. Makes 2 loaves.

MOLASSES RYE BREAD

A woman bakes this superior bread to sell in a craft shop

2 pkgs. active dry yeast	**3 tblsp. brown sugar, firmly**
2 c. lukewarm water	**packed**
2 tblsp. sugar	**2 tblsp. molasses**
3¼ c. sifted flour	**1 tsp. salt**
¼ c. shortening	**2 c. rye flour**

Sprinkle yeast on lukewarm water; stir to dissolve. Add sugar and 2 c. flour. Beat with electric mixer at medium speed until smooth, about 2 minutes, scraping bowl occasionally. Or beat with spoon until batter is smooth. Cover and let rise in warm place until light and bubbly.

Add shortening, brown sugar, molasses, salt and rye flour; beat well. Gradually add enough remaining flour to make a soft dough that leaves the sides of the bowl.

Place dough in lightly greased bowl; turn over to grease top. Cover and let rise in warm place until doubled, about 1 hour.

Punch down. Let rise again until doubled, about 1 hour.

Divide in half. Shape each into a loaf; place in 2 greased 9×5×3″ loaf pans. Let rise until doubled, about 45 minutes.

Bake in 375° oven 30 minutes or until loaves sound hollow when tapped. Remove from pans; cool on racks. Makes 2 loaves.

SWEDISH LIMPA LOAVES

This ribbon winner is a combination of several recipes

⅓ c. brown sugar, firmly packed
¼ c. molasses
2 tblsp. shortening
1 tblsp. salt
1½ c. hot water
1 pkg. active dry yeast
¼ c. lukewarm water
2½ c. rye flour
1 tsp. fennel seeds, crushed
1 tsp. anise seeds, crushed
2 tblsp. grated orange rind
3 c. sifted flour
Melted butter or regular margarine

Combine brown sugar, molasses, shortening, salt and 1½ c. hot water. Cool to lukewarm.

Sprinkle yeast on ¼ c. lukewarm water; stir to dissolve. Add yeast, rye flour, fennel seeds, anise seeds and orange rind to brown sugar mixture. Beat with electric mixer at medium speed until smooth, about 2 minutes, scraping bowl occasionally. Or beat with spoon until batter is smooth.

Gradually add enough flour to make a soft dough that leaves the sides of the bowl. Turn out on floured surface and knead until smooth and satiny, about 10 minutes.

Place dough in lightly greased bowl; turn over to grease top. Cover and let rise in warm place until doubled, about 1½ hours.

Divide dough in half. Shape in balls; let rest 10 minutes. Shape each half into a round loaf and place on 2 greased baking sheets. Press down loaf with palm of hand. Let rise until doubled, about 1 hour. Cut three ¼″ deep slashes on top of each loaf.

Bake in 375° oven 25 to 30 minutes or until loaves sound hollow when tapped. Remove from baking sheets; cool on racks. While still hot, brush with melted butter. Makes 2 loaves.

HIGH-PROTEIN BREAD

The first entry made by this homemaker and a winner

1½ c. creamed cottage cheese	3 pkgs. active dry yeast
1 c. buttermilk	¾ c. lukewarm water
⅓ c. sugar	3 eggs
¼ c. cooking oil	7½ c. sifted flour
4 tsp. salt	Melted butter or regular
¾ tsp. baking soda	margarine

Combine cottage cheese and buttermilk. Heat until lukewarm. Stir in sugar, oil, salt and baking soda.

Sprinkle yeast on lukewarm water; stir to dissolve. Add yeast, eggs and 2 c. flour to buttermilk mixture. Beat with electric mixer at medium speed until smooth, about 2 minutes, scraping bowl occasionally. Or beat with spoon until batter is smooth.

Gradually stir in remaining flour. (Dough will be sticky.) Cover and let rise in warm place until doubled, about 1 hour.

Turn dough out on floured surface and knead until smooth and satiny, about 8 to 10 minutes. Divide dough in thirds. Shape each third into a loaf and place in 3 greased 9×5×3" loaf pans. Let rise until doubled, about 45 minutes.

Bake in 400° oven 30 minutes or until loaves sound hollow when tapped. Remove from pans; cool on racks. While still hot, brush tops with melted butter. Makes 3 loaves.

OATMEAL BREAD

Good, old-fashioned bread with real country flavor

1 c. rolled oats	2 tblsp. melted butter or
2 c. boiling water	regular margarine
2 pkgs. active dry yeast	5 c. sifted flour
⅓ c. lukewarm water	1 egg yolk, beaten
1 tblsp. salt	1 tsp. water
½ c. honey	Poppy seeds

Combine oats with 2 c. boiling water. Let stand 30 minutes.

Sprinkle yeast on ⅓ c. lukewarm water; stir to dissolve. Add yeast, salt, honey, butter and 1 c. flour to oat mixture. Beat with electric mixer at medium speed until smooth, about 2 minutes, scraping bowl occasionally.

Gradually add enough remaining flour to make a soft dough that leaves the sides of the bowl. Turn out on floured surface and knead until smooth and satiny, about 8 to 10 minutes.

Place dough in lightly greased bowl; turn over to grease top. Cover and let rise in warm place until doubled, about 1½ hours.

Divide dough in half. Shape each half into a loaf and place in 2 greased 8½×4½×2½" loaf pans. Let rise until doubled, about 45 minutes.

Brush tops of loaves with combined egg yolk and 1 tsp. water. Sprinkle with poppy seeds.

Bake in 325° oven 50 minutes or until loaves sound hollow when tapped. Remove from pans; cool on racks. Makes 2 loaves.

COTTAGE CHEESE DILL BREAD

Lovely round loaves with the delicate flavor of dill

1 c. cottage cheese	2 tblsp. sugar
1 tblsp. cooking oil	½ c. lukewarm water
1 tblsp. instant onion	2¾ c. sifted flour
1 tsp. dill weed	1 tsp. salt
1 egg	¼ tsp. baking soda
1 pkg. active dry yeast	

Heat cottage cheese until lukewarm. Combine cottage cheese, oil, instant onion, dill weed and egg.

Sprinkle yeast and sugar on lukewarm water; stir to dissolve.

Sift together flour, salt and baking soda.

Add yeast and 1 c. dry ingredients to cottage cheese mixture. Beat with electric mixer at medium speed until smooth, about 2 minutes, scraping bowl occasionally. Or beat with spoon until batter is smooth.

Gradually add remaining flour, stirring well. (Dough will be sticky.) Turn onto lightly floured surface and knead lightly, about 2 minutes. Place dough in greased bowl; turn over to grease top. Cover and let rise until doubled, about 1 hour.

Divide dough in half. Shape each half into round loaf and place on 2 greased baking sheets. Let rise until doubled, about 45 minutes.

Bake in 350° oven 40 minutes or until loaves sound hollow when tapped. Remove from baking sheets; cool on racks. Makes 2 loaves.

ONION CHEESE BREAD

A Purple Ribbon winner at a recent Iowa State Fair

½ c. chopped onion
2 tblsp. butter or regular
   margarine
1 egg, beaten
½ c. milk
1½ c. biscuit mix

½ c. shredded Cheddar
   cheese
2 tsp. parsley flakes
½ c. shredded Cheddar
   cheese

Sauté onion in melted butter in small skillet until tender (do not brown). Set aside to cool.

Combine egg and milk in bowl. Add biscuit mix, stirring just enough to moisten. Stir in cooked onion, ½ c. cheese and parsley flakes. Spread batter in greased 8″ square baking pan. Sprinkle with ½ c. cheese.

Bake in 400° oven 20 minutes or until done. Serve warm. Makes 9 servings.

HERBED BATTER BREAD

Bread can also be baked in 2½-quart ovenproof casserole

1½ c. milk, scalded
3 tblsp. sugar
2 tblsp. butter or regular
   margarine
1 tblsp. salt
¼ c. minced onion

2 pkgs. active dry yeast
½ c. lukewarm water
4½ c. sifted flour
1½ tsp. caraway seeds
½ tsp. ground nutmeg
½ tsp. ground sage

Combine milk, sugar, butter, salt and onion. Cool to luke-warm.

Sprinkle yeast on lukewarm water; stir to dissolve. Add yeast, 2 c. flour, caraway seeds, nutmeg and sage to milk mixture. Beat with electric mixer at medium speed until smooth, about 2 minutes, scraping bowl occasionally. Or beat with spoon until batter is smooth.

Gradually stir in remaining flour. (Dough will be sticky.) Cover and let rise in warm place until doubled, about 1 hour.

Stir batter down by beating with spoon about 25 strokes. Spread in greased 9×5×3″ loaf pan. Let rise until doubled, about 45 minutes.

Bake in 375° oven 1 hour or until loaf sounds hollow when tapped. Remove from pan; cool on rack. Makes 1 loaf.

RYE BATTER BREAD

So easy to prepare . . . you don't have to knead it

1 pkg. active dry yeast
1¼ c. lukewarm water
2 tblsp. honey
2 tblsp. butter or regular
   margarine

2 tsp. salt
1 tblsp. caraway seeds
1 c. rye flour
2½ c. sifted flour

Sprinkle yeast on lukewarm water; stir to dissolve.

Combine yeast, honey, butter, salt, caraway seeds, rye flour and 1 c. flour. Beat with electric mixer at medium speed until smooth, about 2 minutes, scraping bowl occasionally.

Gradually stir in remaining flour. Cover and let rise in warm place until doubled, about 30 minutes.

Stir down by beating with spoon 25 strokes. Spread in greased 9×5×3″ loaf pan. Let rise until doubled, about 40 minutes.

Bake in 375° oven 35 minutes or until loaf sounds hollow when tapped. Remove from pan; cool on rack. Makes 1 loaf.

OUTSTANDING YEAST ROLLS

We selected from ribbon-winning recipes this medley of dinner rolls, golden brown, light and tender. Blue Ribbon Yeast Rolls received the Blue in Washington state and are superior. If you want to impress your guests, serve them Golden Brioche, extra rich and so tender they melt in your mouth.

Our tasters raved about the Cottage Cheese Rolls. This no-knead winner from Illinois is quick, easy and delicious.

Honey Dinner Rolls came away with a Blue Ribbon from a Pennsylvania fair. "I sometimes glaze these rolls with a beaten egg, then top with poppy or caraway seeds and return to oven for 3 minutes—it makes them a bit special for company," the winner told us. We think they are good either way.

BLUE RIBBON YEAST ROLLS

Light and airy rolls you'll be proud to serve any time

½ c. butter or regular margarine	1 c. hot water
⅓ c. sugar	2 pkgs. active dry yeast
1½ tsp. salt	½ c. lukewarm water
2 tblsp. instant potato flakes	4½ c. sifted flour
	Melted butter or regular margarine

Combine butter, sugar, salt, potato flakes and hot water in bowl. Cool to lukewarm.

Sprinkle yeast on lukewarm water; stir to dissolve. Add yeast and 1 c. flour to potato mixture. Beat with electric mixer at medium speed until smooth, about 2 minutes, scraping bowl occasionally. Or beat with spoon until batter is smooth.

Gradually add enough remaining flour to make a soft dough that leaves the sides of the bowl.

Place dough in greased bowl; turn over to grease top. Cover and let rise in warm place until doubled, about 1¼ hours.

Turn dough onto lightly floured surface. Divide dough into 24 equal pieces. Shape each piece into a ball. Place 24 balls in 2 greased 8" square baking pans. Let rise until doubled, about 45 minutes.

Bake in 375° oven 20 minutes or until golden brown. Remove from pans; cool on racks. While still warm, brush with melted butter. Makes 24 rolls.

GOLDEN BRIOCHE

Feathery light rolls that just melt in your mouth

1 pkg. active dry yeast	**1 egg, separated**
¾ c. lukewarm water	**½ c. soft butter or regular**
½ c. sugar	**margarine**
½ tsp. salt	**3½ c. sifted flour**
3 eggs	**1 tblsp. sugar**

Sprinkle yeast on lukewarm water; stir to dissolve.

Combine ½ c. sugar, salt, 3 eggs, 1 egg yolk, butter and 2 c. flour in bowl. Add yeast mixture. Beat with electric mixer at medium speed until smooth, about 2 minutes, scraping bowl occasionally. Or beat with spoon until batter is smooth.

Gradually add remaining flour to make a soft dough that leaves the sides of the bowl. Cover and let rise in warm place until doubled, about 1 hour.

Stir down dough. Cover with plastic wrap. Refrigerate 8 hours or overnight.

Stir down dough. Divide dough into 32 equal pieces. Shape 24 pieces into balls and place in greased muffin-pan cups. Flatten and make a small indention in each with fingers. Cut remaining

8 pieces into 3 equal parts. Shape each into small ball and place in indention. Let rise until doubled, about 1 hour.

Beat together remaining egg white and 1 tblsp. sugar slightly. Brush over rolls.

Bake in 375° oven 18 minutes or until golden. Remove from pans; cool on racks. Makes 24 rolls.

COTTAGE CHEESE ROLLS

Attractive dinner rolls flecked with cottage cheese

2 pkgs. active dry yeast	**2 tsp. salt**
½ c. lukewarm water	**½ tsp. baking soda**
2 c. cottage cheese	**2 eggs**
¼ c. sugar	**4½ c. sifted flour**

Sprinkle yeast on lukewarm water; stir to dissolve.

Heat cottage cheese until lukewarm. Combine cottage cheese, sugar, salt, baking soda, eggs, yeast and 1 c. flour in bowl. Beat with electric mixer at medium speed until smooth, about 2 minutes, scraping bowl occasionally. Or beat with spoon until batter is smooth.

Gradually add enough flour to make a soft dough that leaves the sides of the bowl.

Place dough in greased bowl; turn over to grease top. Cover and let rise in warm place until doubled, about 1½ hours.

Turn dough onto lightly floured surface. Divide dough into 24 equal pieces. Shape each piece into a ball. Place 24 balls in 2 greased 9" round baking pans. Let rise until doubled, about 45 minutes.

Bake in 350° oven 20 minutes or until golden brown. Remove from pans; cool on racks. Makes 24 rolls.

HONEY DINNER ROLLS

For variation, top with sesame seeds before baking

1 c. milk	1 pkg. active dry yeast
¼ c. butter or regular	¼ c. lukewarm water
margarine	4½ c. sifted flour
⅓ c. honey	2 eggs
1 tsp. salt	

Scald milk. Stir in butter, honey and salt. Cool to lukewarm.

Sprinkle yeast on lukewarm water; stir to dissolve. Add yeast, 1 c. flour and eggs to milk mixture. Beat with electric mixer at medium speed until smooth, about 2 minutes, scraping bowl occasionally. Or beat with spoon until batter is smooth.

Gradually add enough flour to make a soft dough that leaves the sides of the bowl. Turn out on floured surface and knead until smooth and satiny, about 8 minutes.

Place dough in greased bowl; turn over to grease top. Cover and let rise in warm place until doubled, about 1 hour.

Divide dough in half. Cut each half into 18 equal pieces. Roll into balls and place in greased 3" muffin-pan cups. Let rise until doubled, about 45 minutes.

Bake in 400° oven 20 minutes or until golden brown. Remove from pans; cool on racks. Makes 36 rolls.

GOLDEN DINNER ROLLS

For a special treat, top with poppy seeds before baking

2 pkgs. active dry yeast	½ c. nonfat dry milk
1 tsp. sugar	1 tblsp. salt
½ c. lukewarm water	½ c. shortening
7 c. sifted flour	2 c. lukewarm water
½ c. sugar	

Sprinkle yeast and 1 tsp. sugar on ½ c. lukewarm water; stir to dissolve.

Combine flour, ½ c. sugar, dry milk and salt in bowl.

Cut in shortening with pastry blender or two knives until mixture resembles coarse crumbs. Make a well in the center. Pour in yeast and 2 c. lukewarm water. Stir until well blended.

Turn onto lightly floured surface and knead until smooth and satiny, about 10 minutes.

Place dough in greased bowl; turn over to grease top. Cover and let rise in a warm place until doubled, about 1½ hours.

Divide dough in quarters. Divide each quarter into 9 equal pieces. Shape each piece into a ball. Place balls in greased 3" muffin-pan cups. Let rise until doubled, about 45 minutes.

Bake in 375° oven 20 minutes or until golden brown. Remove from pans; cool on racks. Makes 36 rolls.

PARKER HOUSE ROLLS

Won a Blue Ribbon in both the county and state fairs

⅓ c. sugar	¼ c. lukewarm water
1 tblsp. shortening	1 egg
1 tsp. salt	4¼ c. sifted flour
1 c. boiling water	Melted butter or regular
1 pkg. active dry yeast	margarine

Combine sugar, shortening, salt and boiling water in bowl. Cool to lukewarm.

Sprinkle yeast on lukewarm water; stir to dissolve. Add yeast, egg and 1 c. flour to water mixture. Beat with electric mixer at medium speed until smooth, about 2 minutes, scraping bowl occasionally. Or beat with spoon until batter is smooth.

Gradually add enough remaining flour to make a soft dough that leaves the sides of the bowl. Cover and let stand 1 hour.

Turn onto lightly floured surface. Roll dough to ½" thickness. Cut with floured 2½" round cookie cutter. Brush with melted butter. Make creases across center of round with edge of knife. Fold so top half overlaps slightly. Press edges together. Brush tops with melted butter. Place on greased baking sheet with sides touching. Let rise until doubled, about 45 minutes.

Bake in 425° oven 15 minutes or until golden brown. Remove from baking sheet; cool on rack. Makes 20 rolls.

LIGHT PUFFY ROLLS

Serve warm with plenty of country fresh butter

3 pkgs. active dry yeast	**1¼ tsp. salt**
2 c. lukewarm water	**1 egg**
½ c. sugar	**7 c. sifted flour**
¼ c. cooking oil	

Sprinkle yeast on lukewarm water; stir to dissolve.

Add sugar, oil, salt and egg; blend well. Let stand 5 minutes. Add 2 c. flour. Beat with electric mixer at medium speed until smooth, about 2 minutes, scraping bowl occasionally. Or beat with spoon until smooth.

Gradually add enough flour to make a soft dough that leaves the sides of the bowl. Turn out on floured surface and knead until smooth and satiny, about 8 minutes.

Place dough in greased bowl; turn over to grease top.

Cover and let rise in warm place until doubled, about 1½ hours.

Divide dough into quarters. Cut each quarter into 18 equal pieces. Roll each piece into a small ball and place two balls in each greased 3″ muffin-pan cup. Let rise until doubled, about 45 minutes.

Bake in 350° oven 20 minutes or until brown. Remove from pans; cool on racks. Makes 36 rolls.

SWEET ROLLS . . . IRRESISTIBLE

All these rolls are so good, it would be difficult to choose which one to try first. For instance, the Sour Cream Cinnamon Rolls, from a Kansas State Fair winner, are a vacation favorite as well as a Blue Ribbon winner. "We never go to the lake in the summertime without taking at least two pans of these rolls. I make and freeze them in disposable pans and my family always asks why I didn't bring another batch," this good cook told us.

You won't be able to stop at one when you bite into a Prune-filled Kolache. "I've been making these for 35 years," the winner from Nebraska said. "There's a saying in our community that in order to be a good Bohemian you must be able to make good kolaches. Well, I am a full-fledged Irish gal married to a Bohemian and I've had wonderful results with this recipe—just follow the directions and you will, too."

SOUR CREAM CINNAMON ROLLS

Serve for supper with sliced luncheon meat and cheese

1 c. dairy sour cream	3 c. sifted flour
2 tblsp. shortening	2 tblsp. soft butter or
½ c. sugar	regular margarine
¼ tsp. baking soda	⅓ c. brown sugar, firmly
1 tsp. salt	packed
1 pkg. active dry yeast	1 tsp. ground cinnamon
¼ c. lukewarm water	Confectioners Sugar Icing
1 egg	(recipe follows)

Heat sour cream in saucepan until lukewarm. Stir in shortening, sugar, baking soda and salt.

Sprinkle yeast on lukewarm water; stir to dissolve. Add yeast and egg to sour cream mixture. Gradually mix in enough flour to make a soft dough.

Turn out on floured surface and knead lightly for a minute. Form into a ball and let rest 5 minutes.

Roll into 13×9″ rectangle. Spread with butter. Sprinkle with brown sugar and cinnamon. Roll up like jelly roll from long side. Cut into 12 slices. Place in greased 13×9×2″ baking pan. Let rise until doubled, about 1½ hours.

Bake in 375° oven 22 minutes or until golden brown. Remove from pan; cool on rack. While warm, drizzle with Confectioners Sugar Icing. Makes 12 rolls.

Confectioners Sugar Icing: Combine 1 c. sifted confectioners sugar, 2 tblsp. light cream or milk and 1 tsp. vanilla; beat until smooth.

PRUNE-FILLED KOLACHES

An original recipe that won first prize in a Nebraska fair

2 c. milk	¼ tsp. ground nutmeg
⅔ c. butter or regular margarine	8 c. sifted flour
¾ c. sugar	Prune Filling (recipe follows)
2 tsp. salt	Crumb Topping (recipe follows)
2 pkgs. active dry yeast	
½ c. lukewarm water	⅓ c. evaporated milk
2 eggs	2 tblsp. sugar
2 tblsp. lemon juice	

Scald milk. Add butter, ¾ c. sugar and salt. Cool to lukewarm. Sprinkle yeast on lukewarm water; stir to dissolve.

Add yeast, eggs, lemon juice, nutmeg and 2 c. flour to milk mixture. Beat with electric mixer at medium speed until smooth, about 2 minutes, scraping bowl occasionally.

Turn dough onto floured surface; let rest 10 minutes.

Knead dough until smooth and satiny, about 10 minutes. Place dough in greased bowl; turn over to grease top. Let rise in warm place until doubled, about 1½ hours.

Prepare Prune Filling and Crumb Topping.

Divide dough into quarters. Divide each quarter into 12 equal pieces. Shape each piece into a smooth ball. Place balls about 3″ apart on greased baking sheets. Press down each ball with palm to flatten. Make a deep indentation in the center of each ball. Fill with 1 tsp. of Prune Filling. Sprinkle with Crumb Topping. Let rise until doubled, about 45 minutes.

Bake in 375° oven 15 minutes or until golden brown. While hot, brush rolls with combined evaporated milk and 2 tblsp. sugar. Remove from baking sheets; cool on racks. Makes 48 rolls.

Prune Filling: Place 1 lb. pitted prunes in a medium saucepan with enough water to cover. Bring to a boil; reduce heat and simmer until prunes are tender. Remove from heat; drain well. While hot, mash prunes until smooth. Add 1 tblsp. lemon juice, 1 c. sugar, 2 tblsp. flour, ¼ c. butter or regular margarine, ¼ tsp. ground cinnamon, 1 tsp. vanilla and dash salt; stir well. Cook over medium heat, stirring constantly, until mixture is thickened. Cool completely.

Crumb Topping: Combine ½ c. flour and ½ c. sugar in bowl. Cut in ¼ c. butter or regular margarine with pastry blender or two knives until mixture is crumbly.

BLUE RIBBON CINNAMON ROLLS

Makes two pans to extra-large cinnamon-swirled buns

2 pkgs. active dry yeast
3 c. lukewarm water
½ c. butter or regular margarine
¼ c. shortening
¾ c. sugar
2 tsp. salt
2 eggs
10 c. sifted flour

1 c. maple-flavored syrup
½ c. butter or regular margarine
1 c. brown sugar, firmly packed
Melted butter or regular margarine
Ground cinnamon

Sprinkle yeast on lukewarm water; stir to dissolve.

Add ½ c. butter, shortening, sugar, salt, eggs and 2 c. flour. Beat with electric mixer at medium speed until smooth, about 2 minutes, scraping bowl occasionally. Or beat with spoon until batter is smooth.

Gradually add enough remaining flour to make a soft dough that leaves the sides of the bowl. Place dough in lightly greased bowl; turn over to grease top. Cover and let rise in warm place until doubled, about 1½ hours.

Combine syrup, ½ c. butter and brown sugar in saucepan. Heat until sugar dissolves, stirring occasionally. Remove from heat. Cool to lukewarm. Pour syrup mixture evenly into two 13×9×2" baking pans.

Divide dough in half. Roll each into 14×12" rectangle on

floured surface. Spread with melted butter. Sprinkle with cinnamon. Roll up like jelly roll from narrow side. Cut into 12 slices. Place in 1 prepared pan. Repeat with remaining dough. Let rise until doubled, about 45 minutes.

Bake in 375° oven 30 minutes or until golden brown. Remove from pans; cool on racks over waxed paper. Makes 24 rolls.

ORANGE BREAKFAST ROLLS

Attractive rolls with a tangy orange marmalade icing

¾ c. milk	2 tblsp. cornstarch
½ c. sugar	4 c. sifted flour
¼ c. butter or regular	2 eggs
margarine	¼ c. grated orange rind
1 tsp. salt	Orange Marmalade Icing
2 pkgs. active dry yeast	(recipe follows)
½ c. lukewarm water	

Scald milk. Stir in sugar, butter and salt. Cool to lukewarm.

Sprinkle yeast on lukewarm water; stir to dissolve. Add yeast, cornstarch, 1 c. flour, eggs and orange rind to milk mixture. Beat with electric mixer at medium speed until smooth, about 2 minutes, scraping bowl occasionally. Or beat with spoon until batter is smooth.

Gradually add remaining flour, stirring to make a stiff batter. Cover with plastic wrap. Chill 1 hour.

Roll dough into 18×10" rectangle on floured surface. Cut crosswise in 36 strips, ½" wide. Twist each strip. Coil into rounds on greased baking sheets. Let rise until doubled, about 1 hour.

Bake in 375° oven 12 minutes or until golden brown. Remove from baking sheets; cool on racks. While warm, frost with Orange Marmalade Icing. Makes 36 rolls.

Orange Marmalade Icing: Combine 2 c. sifted confectioners sugar, ¼ c. orange marmalade and 2 tblsp. evaporated milk. Stir until smooth.

BUTTERY WALNUT ROLLS

Light-textured rolls well worth the time and effort

4¼ c. sifted flour
½ c. sugar
2 tblsp. cornstarch
1 tsp. salt
¾ c. milk
¼ c. butter or regular
   margarine
2 pkgs. active dry yeast
½ c. lukewarm water
2 eggs

1 c. butter or regular
   margarine
Melted butter or regular
   margarine
½ c. sugar
1 tsp. ground cinnamon
¾ c. chopped walnuts
Thin White Icing (recipe
   follows)

Combine 2 c. flour, ½ c. sugar, cornstarch and salt in bowl. Scald milk. Add ¼ c. butter; cool to lukewarm.

Sprinkle yeast on lukewarm water; stir to dissolve. Add yeast, eggs and milk mixture to dry ingredients. Beat with electric mixer at medium speed until smooth, about 2 minutes, scraping bowl occasionally. Or beat with spoon until batter is smooth.

Gradually add enough flour to make a soft dough that leaves the sides of the bowl. Cover with plastic wrap. Chill in refrigerator 1 hour.

Turn dough on lightly floured surface. Roll into 18×12″ rectangle. Dot surface with ⅓ c. butter cut in small pieces. Fold rectangle into thirds, making three layers. Wrap with plastic wrap. Chill in refrigerator 15 minutes. Repeat rolling and folding procedure 2 more times, using ⅓ c. butter each time. Wrap securely with plastic wrap. Refrigerate overnight.

Roll dough into 18×10″ rectangle on floured surface. Cut in half lengthwise. Cut each half into 16 strips. Dip each strip in melted butter and then in combined ½ c. sugar, cinnamon and walnuts. Twist strip and shape into a coil. Place in 2 greased 9″ square baking pans. (Put 16 strips into each pan.) Let rise until doubled, about 45 minutes.

Bake in 375° oven 20 minutes or until golden brown. Remove

from pans; cool on racks. While still warm, drizzle with Thin White Icing. Makes 32 rolls.

Thin White Icing: Combine 1 c. sifted confectioners sugar, ½ tsp. vanilla and 1 tblsp. water; stir until smooth.

ORANGE-FROSTED BOWKNOTS

Tangy orange frosting makes these rolls a real treat

1 c. milk	¼ c. lukewarm water
½ c. butter or regular margarine	2 eggs
½ c. sugar	5 c. sifted flour
1½ tsp. salt	2 tsp. grated orange rind
¼ c. orange juice	Orange Icing (recipe
1 pkg. active dry yeast	follows)

Scald milk. Stir in butter, sugar, salt and orange juice. Cool to lukewarm.

Sprinkle yeast on lukewarm water; stir to dissolve. Add yeast, eggs, 2 c. flour and orange rind to milk mixture. Beat with electric mixer at medium speed until smooth, about 2 minutes, scraping bowl occasionally. Or beat with spoon until batter is smooth.

Gradually add enough remaining flour to make a soft dough that leaves the sides of the bowl. Cover; let rest 10 minutes.

Turn out on floured surface and knead until smooth and satiny, about 8 to 10 minutes.

Place dough in greased bowl; turn over to grease top. Cover and let rise in warm place until doubled, about 1½ hours.

Divide dough in half. Roll each into 11×8" rectangle on floured surface. Cut into 22 (½") strips. Tie into bows and place on greased baking sheets. Let rise until doubled, about 45 minutes.

Bake in 350° oven 12 minutes or golden brown. Remove from baking sheets; cool on racks. Frost with Orange Icing. Makes 44 rolls.

Orange Icing: Combine 2 c. sifted confectioners sugar, 2 tsp. grated orange rind and ¼ c. orange juice. Mix until smooth.

HOT CROSS BUNS

Special Easter rolls that are good any season of the year

½ c. sugar	¼ c. water
1 pkg. active dry yeast	1 egg
½ tsp. ground cinnamon	1 c. raisins
¼ tsp. salt	¼ c. candied orange peel
4½ c. sifted flour	1 egg yolk, beaten
1 c. milk	2 tsp. water
½ c. butter or regular margarine	

Combine sugar, yeast, cinnamon, salt and 1 c. flour in bowl.

Heat milk, butter and ¼ c. water until lukewarm. (Butter does not have to be completely melted.) Gradually pour liquid into dry ingredients, beating with electric mixer at low speed about 2 minutes, scraping bowl occasionally. Add egg and 1 c. flour, beat for 2 more minutes, scraping bowl occasionally. Or beat with spoon until batter is smooth.

Gradually add enough remaining flour to make a soft dough that leaves the sides of the bowl. Turn out on floured surface and knead 5 minutes. Add raisins and orange peel and continue kneading until smooth and satiny, about 5 minutes.

Place dough in lightly greased bowl; turn over to grease top. Cover and let rise in warm place until doubled, about 2 hours.

Punch down. Shape into a ball; let rest 15 minutes.

Divide dough into 12 equal pieces. Shape each into a ball. Place balls in greased 13×9×2″ baking pan. Brush with combined egg yolk and 2 tsp. water. Snip a cross on top of each bun with scissors. Let rise until doubled, about 30 minutes.

Bake in 350° oven 30 minutes or until golden brown. Remove from pan; cool on rack. Prepare your favorite confectioners sugar icing and spread on crosses. Makes 12 rolls.

REFRIGERATOR BUTTERSCOTCH ROLLS

The topping makes these rolls unusual as well as luscious

¾ c. milk
½ c. butter or regular
   margarine
½ c. sugar
2 tsp. salt
2 pkgs. active dry yeast
½ c. lukewarm water
1 egg

4 c. sifted flour
Butterscotch Topping
   (recipe follows)
Melted butter or regular
   margarine
½ c. sugar
2 tsp. ground cinnamon

Scald milk. Stir in butter, ½ c. sugar and salt. Cool to luke-warm.

Sprinkle yeast on lukewarm water; stir to dissolve. Add yeast, egg and 1 c. flour to milk mixture. Beat with electric mixer at medium speed until smooth, about 2 minutes, scraping bowl occasionally. Or beat with spoon until batter is smooth.

Gradually add enough remaining flour to make a soft dough that leaves the sides of the bowl. Cover with plastic wrap. Refrigerate at least 2 hours or overnight.

Prepare Butterscotch Topping.

Roll into 18×12″ rectangle on floured surface. Brush with melted butter. Sprinkle with a mixture of ½ c. sugar and cinnamon. Roll up like jelly roll from long side. Cut into 18 slices. Place in prepared pans. Let rise until doubled, about 1 hour.

Bake in 375° oven 30 minutes or until golden brown. Remove from pans; cool on racks over waxed paper. Makes 18 rolls.

Butterscotch Topping: Combine ¼ c. light corn syrup, 2 tblsp. butter or regular margarine and 1 tblsp. water in small saucepan. Bring to a boil, stirring constantly. Boil 1 minute. Remove from heat. Add 1 (6 oz.) pkg. butterscotch-flavored pieces; stir until melted. Pour mixture evenly into two 9″ square baking pans. Sprinkle with ⅔ c. chopped pecans.

VERY BEST QUICK BREADS AND BISCUITS

A Blue Ribbon winner from Missouri wrote us "What could be better for breakfast than hot flaky biscuits with homemade jam or jelly—My Make-ahead Biscuit Mix is so quick and easy that I serve these at least three times a week."

From an Iowa Blue Ribbon winner we obtained her specialty, Honey Corn Bread. "The flavor of honey really comes through; we serve it with lots of butter and honey," she told us.

"I won a Blue Ribbon at the North Carolina Fair with my Luscious Cornmeal Bars," a farm woman wrote us—"but I also bake this in a ring mold and then fill the center with creamed vegetables. It's one of our favorite suppers along with tomato salad and big glasses of frosty cold buttermilk."

LUSCIOUS CORNMEAL BARS

A good choice for lunch . . . serve with a green salad

1½ c. chopped onion	¼ lb. ground beef, cooked
3 tblsp. butter or regular	and drained (1 c.)
margarine	1 tsp. parsley flakes
1 c. sifted flour	2 eggs, beaten
1 c. cornmeal	1 c. milk
3 tsp. baking powder	1½ c. shredded sharp
1 tsp. salt	Cheddar cheese
⅓ c. butter or regular	
margarine	

Sauté onion in 3 tblsp. melted butter in small skillet until tender (do not brown). Set aside to cool.

Sift together flour, cornmeal, baking powder and salt into bowl. Cut in ⅓ c. butter with pastry blender or two knives until mixture resembles coarse meal. Add 2 tblsp. cooked onion, cooked ground beef and parsley flakes.

Combine eggs and milk. Add to dry ingredients, stirring just enough to moisten. Spread batter in well-greased 11×7×1½" baking dish. Spoon remaining onion on top of batter. Sprinkle with cheese.

Bake in 425° oven 20 minutes or until done. Serve warm. Makes 10 servings.

HONEY CORN BREAD

Serve large squares of this with thick, hearty chili

1 c. sifted flour	¼ c. honey
¾ c. cornmeal	2 tblsp. melted butter or
3 tsp. baking powder	regular margarine
½ tsp. salt	1 c. milk
1 egg, beaten	

Sift together flour, cornmeal, baking powder and salt into bowl.

Combine egg, honey, butter and milk. Add to dry ingredients, stirring just enough to moisten. Pour batter into greased 8" square baking pan.

Bake in 400° oven 30 minutes or until done. Serve warm with honey, if you wish. Makes 9 servings.

ZUCCHINI NUT BREAD

Wrap tightly and let mellow overnight before slicing

3 c. sifted flour	1 c. cooking oil
1½ tsp. ground cinnamon	1 tblsp. vanilla
1 tsp. baking soda	2 c. grated, unpared
1 tsp. salt	zucchini squash
¼ tsp. baking powder	½ c. chopped walnuts
3 eggs	1 tsp. flour
2 c. sugar	

Sift together flour, cinnamon, baking soda, salt and baking powder.

Beat eggs well. Gradually add sugar and oil, mixing well. Add vanilla and dry ingredients; blend well. Stir in zucchini.

Combine walnuts with 1 tsp. flour; stir into batter. Pour into 2 greased 8½ ×4½ ×2½″ loaf pans.

Bake in 350° oven 1 hour or until bread tests done. Cool in pans on racks 10 minutes. Remove from pans; cool on racks. Makes 2 loaves.

MAKE-AHEAD BISCUIT MIX

Such a timesaver . . . hot biscuits in minutes

9 c. sifted flour
1 c. nonfat dry milk
⅓ c. baking powder

4 tsp. salt
1¾ c. shortening

Stir together flour, dry milk, baking powder and salt in large bowl. Cut in shortening with pastry blender or two knives until mixture resembles coarse meal. Store in airtight container in a cool place. Makes about 12 cups.

To Make Basic Biscuits: Combine 2 c. Make-ahead Biscuit Mix and ½ c. water. Mix with fork just enough to make a soft dough that sticks together.

Turn onto lightly floured surface and knead lightly 15 times. Roll to ½″ thickness. Cut with floured 2″ cutter and place about 1″ apart on ungreased baking sheet.

Bake in 425° oven 12 minutes or until golden brown. Serve immediately. Makes 10.

MILE-HIGH BISCUITS

Stack a napkin-lined basket with these tempting biscuits

3 c. sifted flour
2 tblsp. sugar
4½ tsp. baking powder
¾ tsp. cream of tartar

¾ tsp. salt
¾ c. shortening
1 egg, beaten
1 c. milk

Sift together flour, sugar, baking powder, cream of tartar and salt into bowl.

Cut in shortening with pastry blender or two knives until mixture resembles coarse meal.

Combine egg and milk. Add to flour mixture all at once, stirring just enough with fork to make a soft dough that sticks together.

Turn onto lightly floured surface and knead lightly 15 times. Roll to 1" thickness. Cut with floured 2" cutter and place about 1" apart on ungreased baking sheet.

Bake in 450° oven 12 to 15 minutes or until golden brown. Serve immediately. Makes 16.

FLAKY BAKING POWDER BISCUITS

Always a favorite served with homemade jam or jelly

2 c. sifted flour	½ c. shortening
1 tblsp. sugar	1 egg, beaten
4 tsp. baking powder	⅔ c. milk
½ tsp. salt	

Sift together flour, sugar, baking powder and salt into bowl.

Cut in shortening with pastry blender or two knives until mixture resembles coarse meal. Combine egg and milk. Add to flour mixture all at once, stirring just enough with fork to make a soft dough that sticks together.

Turn onto lightly floured surface and knead lightly 15 times. Roll to ¾" thickness. Cut with floured 2" cutter and place about 1" apart on ungreased baking sheet.

Bake in 425° oven 12 minutes or until golden brown. Serve immediately. Makes 16.

FABULOUS FRUIT AND NUT QUICK BREADS

Purple Ribbon Prune Bread from an outstanding cook in Idaho has won a flutter of Blue and Purple Ribbons. Copied from her mother's treasured recipe files, this dark spicy bread would make a delightful homemade Christmas gift.

Grandma's Banana Bread has captured five Blue Ribbons so far. Baked in a 9-inch tube pan, crunchy with pecans and mellow banana flavor, it's a company special.

"Christmas wouldn't be the same without Cranberry Nut Bread," a West Virginia homemaker told us. "I always bake several ahead and freeze. When friends drop by I cut it into thin slices and serve with fruit punch or hot coffee—everyone looks forward to it." After tasting it we know why this golden beauty studded with ruby flecks of cranberries won.

PURPLE RIBBON PRUNE BREAD

"A favorite from Mom's collection of bread recipes"

1-28-93
good
grade
8

1½ c. chopped prunes	⅓ c. honey
1 c. boiling water	1 egg, beaten
2½ c. sifted flour	1 tsp. vanilla
⅔ c. sugar	2 tblsp. cooking oil
1 tsp. baking soda	1 tsp. grated orange rind
1 tsp. salt	1 c. chopped walnuts
1 tsp. ground cinnamon	1 tblsp. flour
½ tsp. ground nutmeg	

Combine prunes and boiling water; cover and let stand 20 minutes.

Sift together 2½ c. flour, sugar, baking soda, salt, cinnamon and nutmeg into bowl.

Add honey, egg and vanilla to prunes; mix well. Add prune mixture, oil and orange rind to dry ingredients; stir just until moistened.

Combine walnuts with 1 tblsp. flour; stir into batter. Pour into greased 9×5×3" loaf pan.

Bake in 325° oven 1 hour and 10 minutes or until bread tests done. Cool in pan on rack 10 minutes. Remove from pan; cool on rack. Makes 1 loaf.

GRANDMA'S BANANA BREAD

Unusual-shaped breakfast bread . . . good with whipped butter

2 c. sifted flour
2 tsp. baking soda
1 tsp. ground cinnamon
½ tsp. salt
½ tsp. ground nutmeg
½ c. shortening

1 c. sugar
2 eggs
1 tsp. vanilla
1 c. mashed bananas
½ c. chopped pecans
1 tsp. flour

Sift together 2 c. flour, baking soda, cinnamon, salt and nutmeg.

Cream together shortening and sugar. Blend in eggs and vanilla; mix well. Add dry ingredients alternately with bananas, mixing just until blended.

Combine pecans and 1 tsp. flour; stir into batter. Pour into greased 9″ tube pan.

Bake in 350° oven 45 to 50 minutes or until bread tests done. Cool in pan on rack 10 minutes. Remove from pan; cool on rack. Makes 1 loaf.

CRANBERRY NUT BREAD

Serve with a fruit salad for dessert during the holidays

2 c. sifted flour
1 c. sugar
1½ tsp. baking powder
1 tsp. salt
½ tsp. baking soda
¼ c. shortening
1 egg, beaten

¾ c. orange juice
1 tblsp. grated orange rind
1 c. coarsely chopped
   cranberries
¼ c. chopped walnuts
1 tblsp. flour

Sift together 2 c. flour, sugar, baking powder, salt and baking soda in bowl. Cut in shortening until mixture resembles coarse meal. Combine egg, orange juice and orange rind in small bowl. Add to dry ingredients all at once; stir just until moistened.

Combine cranberries, walnuts and 1 tblsp. flour; stir into batter. Pour into greased and waxed-paper-lined 9×5×3″ loaf pan.

Bake in 350° oven 1 hour or until bread tests done. Cool in pan on rack 10 minutes. Remove from pan; cool on rack. Makes 1 loaf.

BLUEBERRY LEMON BREAD

Delicious when made with fresh juicy blueberries

3 c. sifted flour
4 tsp. baking powder
1½ tsp. salt
2 eggs
1 c. sugar
1 c. milk
3 tblsp. melted shortening

1 tsp. vanilla
1 tsp. grated lemon rind
1 (10 oz.) pkg. frozen blueberries, thawed and drained (1 c.)
½ c. chopped walnuts
1 tblsp. flour

Sift together 3 c. flour, baking powder and salt.

Beat eggs well; gradually beat in sugar.

Combine milk and shortening; add to egg mixture. Add vanilla and lemon rind. Add dry ingredients; stir to blend. Stir in combined blueberries, walnuts and 1 tblsp. flour. Pour into greased 9×5×3″ loaf pan.

Bake in 350° oven 1 hour or until bread tests done. Cool in pan on rack 10 minutes. Remove from pan; cool on rack. Makes 1 loaf.

PINEAPPLE NUT BREAD

Freeze several of these ahead for holiday entertaining

2 c. sifted flour
1 tsp. baking powder
1 tsp. baking soda
½ tsp. salt
2 tblsp. shortening
½ c. sugar

1 egg
1 tsp. vanilla
1 (8½ oz.) can crushed pineapple
½ c. chopped walnuts
½ c. raisins

Sift together flour, baking powder, baking soda and salt.

Cream together shortening and sugar until light and fluffy. Add egg and vanilla; beat well. Add dry ingredients alternately with undrained pineapple; stir to moisten. Stir in walnuts and raisins. Pour into greased 9×5×3″ loaf pan.

Bake in 350° oven 1 hour or until bread tests done. Cool in pan on rack 10 minutes. Remove from pan; cool on rack. Makes 1 loaf.

ORANGE NUT LOAF

A golden brown loaf studded with chopped dates and walnuts

2 c. sifted flour	1 egg, beaten
2 tsp. baking powder	½ c. sugar
½ tsp. baking soda	2 tblsp. melted butter or
½ tsp. salt	regular margarine
½ c. chopped walnuts	⅓ c. orange juice
1 tblsp. grated orange rind	⅔ c. water
⅔ c. cut-up dates	1 tsp. vanilla

Sift together flour, baking powder, baking soda and salt. Stir in walnuts, orange rind and dates.

Combine egg, sugar, butter, orange juice, water and vanilla; blend well. Add dry ingredients all at once; stir just until moistened. Pour into greased 8½ ×4½ ×2½″ loaf pan. Let stand 20 minutes.

Bake in 325° oven 55 minutes or until bread tests done. Cool in pan on rack 10 minutes. Remove from pan; cool on rack. Makes 1 loaf.

ORANGE WALNUT BREAD

"An heirloom from Grandmother that is still a winner today"

2 c. sifted flour	1 tblsp. flour
1 tsp. baking powder	1 egg, beaten
½ tsp. baking soda	1 c. sugar
½ tsp. salt	2 tblsp. melted butter or
¾ c. finely chopped dates	regular margarine
1½ tsp. grated orange rind	¾ c. orange juice
¾ c. chopped walnuts	

Sift together 2 c. flour, baking powder, baking soda and salt in bowl.

Combine dates, orange rind and walnuts with 1 tblsp. flour.

Combine egg, sugar, butter and orange juice; blend well. Stir into dry ingredients, blending well. Stir in date mixture. Pour into greased 8½ ×4½ ×2½ " loaf pan.

Bake in 350° oven 1 hour or until done. Cool in pan on rack 10 minutes. Remove from pan; cool on rack. Makes 1 loaf.

DELICIOUS DATE WALNUT LOAF

Won a Blue Ribbon in the nut bread division in Montana

2 c. sifted flour	1 c. boiling water
1½ tsp. salt	⅓ c. cold water
1 tsp. baking powder	¾ c. brown sugar, firmly
1 tsp. baking soda	packed
2 c. chopped dates	1 tsp. vanilla
1 c. chopped walnuts	1 egg
⅓ c. shortening	

Sift together flour, salt, baking powder and baking soda.

Combine dates, walnuts and shortening in bowl. Add boiling water and beat with a wooden spoon until shortening breaks in small lumps. Add cold water.

Stir in brown sugar, vanilla and egg; mix well. Add dry ingredients; beat well. Pour into greased 9×5×3" loaf pan.

Bake in 350° oven 1 hour and 15 minutes or until bread tests done. Cool in pan on rack 10 minutes. Remove from pan; cool on rack. Makes 1 loaf.

GOLDEN BANANA NUT LOAF

An exceptional golden brown loaf that will please your family

3 c. sifted flour	1 egg
3½ tsp. baking powder	1 c. mashed bananas
1 tsp. salt	¾ c. milk
2 tblsp. shortening	¾ c. chopped walnuts
1 c. sugar	1 tblsp. flour

Sift together 3 c. flour, baking powder and salt.

Cream together shortening and sugar until light and fluffy. Add egg; beat well. Beat in bananas and milk. Gradually add dry ingredients; mix just until moistened.

Combine walnuts and 1 tblsp. flour; stir into batter. Pour into greased 9×5×3″ loaf pan. Let stand 20 minutes.

Bake in 350° oven 1 hour and 10 minutes or until bread tests done. Cool in pan on rack 10 minutes. Remove from pan; cool on rack. Makes 1 loaf.

BANANA WALNUT BREAD

This mild-flavored loaf slices better after 24 hours

1¾ c. sifted flour	½ c. sugar
2 tsp. baking powder	2 eggs
½ tsp. salt	1 c. mashed bananas
¼ tsp. baking soda	½ c. chopped walnuts
⅓ c. shortening	1 tblsp. flour

6-18-92 Grade 5

Sift together 1¾ c. flour, baking powder, salt and baking soda.

Cream together shortening and sugar until light and fluffy. Add eggs, one at a time, beating well after each addition. Add dry ingredients alternately with bananas, beating after each addition.

Combine walnuts and 1 tblsp. flour; stir into batter. Pour into greased 9×5×3″ loaf pan.

Bake in 350° oven 1 hour or until bread tests done. Cool in pan on rack 10 minutes. Remove from pan; cool on rack. Makes 1 loaf.

MUFFINS YOU'LL WANT TO MAKE AGAIN AND AGAIN

If you like your muffins plain as does one farmer who said, "I like a good plain muffin—nothing fancy," then stir up a batch of Basic Sweet Muffins that a Kansas family have been eating for 32 years. Or make the Plain Muffins that won a Blue at a New York fair—"though I sometimes drop a teaspoon of blackberry jam in center of each muffin before baking. My Grandmother used this recipe since she was a bride, claimed it was the only thing she didn't burn or ruin when she was learning to cook," this winner told us.

We also include three great breakfast muffins—Whole Wheat Granola from Nebraska—made with whole wheat flour, Granola, raisins, Oatmeal Muffins from Pennsylvania with just a hint of cinnamon in the batter and High-Protein Muffins from Arizona, chock-full of nutrients—wheat germ, raisins, honey, whole wheat flour and a whisper of nutmeg.

BASIC SWEET MUFFINS

A 4-H member has won several ribbons with this recipe

1¾ c. sifted flour	½ c. butter or regular
¼ c. sugar	margarine
3 tsp. baking powder	1 egg, beaten
½ tsp. salt	¾ c. milk

Sift together flour, sugar, baking powder and salt into bowl.

Cut in butter with pastry blender or two knives until mixture resembles cornmeal.

Combine egg and milk. Add to dry mixture, stirring just enough to moisten. Spoon batter into greased 3″ muffin-pan cups, filling two-thirds full.

Bake in 400° oven 20 minutes or until done. Makes 12.

PLAIN MUFFINS

Stir in 1 c. currants or blueberries for a change

2 c. sifted flour	1 egg, beaten
3 tblsp. sugar	3 tblsp. melted butter or
2 tsp. baking powder	regular margarine
½ tsp. salt	1 c. milk

Sift together flour, sugar, baking powder and salt into bowl.

Combine egg, butter and milk. Add to dry ingredients, stirring just enough to moisten. Spoon batter into greased 2½" muffin-pan cups, filling two-thirds full.

Bake in 400° oven 25 minutes or until done. Makes 12.

GOLDEN CORNMEAL MUFFINS

"The best cornmeal muffins we've made," our testers said

1½ c. sifted flour	2 eggs, beaten
¾ c. cornmeal	3 tblsp. melted butter or
½ c. sugar	regular margarine
4 tsp. baking powder	1 c. milk
1 tsp. salt	

Sift together flour, cornmeal, sugar, baking powder and salt into bowl.

Combine eggs, butter and milk. Add to dry ingredients, stirring just enough to moisten. Spoon batter into greased 3" muffin-pan cups, filling two-thirds full.

Bake in 400° oven 15 minutes or until done. Makes 12.

WHOLE WHEAT GRANOLA MUFFINS

An excellent muffin, chock-full of nutrients

1¾ c. sifted flour	½ c. whole wheat flour
3 tsp. baking powder	1 egg, beaten
¼ tsp. salt	¼ c. cooking oil
1 c. Granola	1 c. milk
½ c. brown sugar, firmly	¼ c. raisins
packed	1 tsp. flour

Sift together 1¾ c. flour, baking powder and salt into bowl. Stir in Granola, brown sugar and whole wheat flour.

Combine egg, oil and milk. Add to dry ingredients, stirring just enough to moisten. Stir in combined raisins and 1 tsp. flour. Spoon batter into greased 2½" muffin-pan cups, filling two-thirds full.

Bake in 400° oven 20 minutes or until done. Makes 12.

OATMEAL MUFFINS

These golden muffins are the perfect choice for brunch

1 c. sifted flour
2 tsp. baking powder
½ tsp. baking soda
½ tsp. salt
½ tsp. ground cinnamon
1 c. quick-cooking oats

½ c. brown sugar, firmly
   packed
1 c. buttermilk
1 egg, beaten
¼ c. cooking oil

Sift together flour, baking powder, baking soda, salt and cinnamon.

Combine oats, brown sugar and buttermilk in bowl; let stand 10 minutes. Add egg and oil; mix well. Add dry ingredients, stirring just enough to moisten. Spoon batter into greased 2½″ muffin-pan cups, filling two-thirds full.

Bake in 375° oven 25 minutes or until done. Makes 12.

HIGH-PROTEIN MUFFINS

Moist muffins with a nutty whole grain flavor

2½ c. bran flakes
1½ c. raisins
1¾ c. milk
1 c. whole wheat flour
1 c. soy flour
1 c. toasted wheat germ
4 tsp. baking powder

1½ tsp. ground nutmeg
¾ tsp. salt
4 eggs
⅔ c. honey
⅔ c. cooking oil
¼ c. dark molasses

Combine bran flakes, raisins and milk in bowl; set aside.

Stir together whole wheat flour, soy flour, wheat germ, baking powder, nutmeg and salt. Beat together eggs, honey, oil and molasses. Add egg mixture to soaked bran flakes; mix well.

Add dry ingredients all at once, stirring just enough to moisten. Spoon batter into paper-lined 3″ muffin-pan cups, filling two-thirds full.

Bake in 350° oven 25 minutes or until done. Makes 30.

CORNMEAL SURPRISE MUFFINS

Any favorite jam or jelly can be used in these muffins

1 c. sifted flour
1 c. cornmeal
2 tblsp. sugar
3 tsp. baking powder
½ tsp. salt

1 egg, beaten
1 c. milk
3 tblsp. cooking oil
Red raspberry or currant
jelly

Sift together flour, cornmeal, sugar, baking powder and salt into bowl. Combine egg, milk and oil. Add to dry ingredients, stirring just enough to moisten. Spoon batter into greased 3″ muffin-pan cups, filling one-half full. Place a teaspoon of jelly in center of each. Top with enough batter to fill two-thirds full.

Bake in 425° oven 20 minutes or until done. Makes 10.

GRAHAM MUFFINS

This homemaker wins several ribbons every year in Wisconsin

1½ c. graham cracker
crumbs
2 tsp. baking powder
⅓ c. melted butter or
regular margarine

¼ c. dark corn syrup
1 egg, beaten
½ c. milk
½ c. chopped pecans
1 tblsp. flour

Combine graham cracker crumbs and baking powder in bowl. Combine butter, corn syrup, egg and milk. Add to graham cracker mixture, stirring just enough to moisten. Stir in combined pecans and flour. Spoon batter into greased 3″ muffin-pan cups, filling two-thirds full.

Bake in 375° oven 20 minutes or until done. Makes 12.

DELICIOUS DOUGHNUTS FROM THE FAIRS

Every one of these doughnuts is downright delicious eating, and each is different. Maple-frosted Doughnuts, cut in rectangles are superb. "My husband is responsible for my Blue Ribbon," the Oregon woman wrote us. "He saw maple-frosted rectangular doughnuts in a bakery and suggested that I try to duplicate the recipe. I experimented until I had a light puffy doughnut—used a Spam can to cut the shape and put maple extract in the icing. The final result was twice as good as the bakery product, my husband told me."

A Blue Ribbon winner from Montana, Golden Doughnut Puffs, are crusty on the outside and feather-light inside with a nice tang of lemon flavor.

"Light and airy" describes the Puffy Potato Doughnuts from a good Wyoming cook, who told us that these doughnuts always win a Purple Ribbon when she enters them in the state fair. "The recipe makes a large batch so I freeze half of them."

"My Best-ever Doughnuts have won me the most ribbons through the years and I've been competing in fairs over 50 years," said a farm homemaker from Missouri.

MAPLE-FROSTED DOUGHNUTS

An Oregon woman developed this recipe for her husband

1 c. milk	1 egg
2 tblsp. shortening	3 c. sifted flour
2 tblsp. sugar	Cooking oil
1 tsp. salt	Maple Frosting (recipe
1 pkg. active dry yeast	follows)
¼ c. lukewarm water	

Scald milk. Stir in shortening, sugar and salt. Cool to lukewarm.

Sprinkle yeast on lukewarm water; stir to dissolve. Add yeast, egg and 1 c. flour to milk mixture. Beat with electric mixer at medium speed until smooth, about 2 minutes, scraping bowl occasionally. Or beat with spoon until batter is smooth.

Gradually add remaining flour, blending well. Cover and let rise in warm place until doubled, about 1 hour.

Roll out dough ¼" thick on floured surface. Cut with floured knife into 3×1½" bars. Place on floured waxed paper. Cover and let rise until doubled, about 45 minutes.

Fry a few doughnuts at a time in hot cooking oil (375°) until golden brown, turning once. Drain on paper towels. When cool, spread with Maple Frosting. Makes about 3 dozen.

Maple Frosting: Combine 2 c. sifted confectioners sugar, ½ c. soft butter or regular margarine, ½ tsp. maple flavoring and enough hot water to make a creamy frosting. Beat until smooth.

GOLDEN DOUGHNUT PUFFS

One of the best doughnuts we've tested in our Kitchens

1 c. milk, scalded	2 eggs
½ c. butter or regular margarine	1 tsp. grated lemon rind
	1 tsp. lemon juice
⅔ c. sugar	6½ c. sifted flour
1 tsp. salt	Cooking oil
3 pkgs. active dry yeast	Sugar
1 c. lukewarm water	

Combine milk, butter, ⅔ c. sugar and salt. Cool to lukewarm.

Sprinkle yeast on lukewarm water; stir to dissolve. Add yeast, eggs, lemon rind, lemon juice and 1 c. flour to milk mixture. Beat with electric mixer at medium speed until smooth, about 2 minutes, scraping bowl occasionally. Or beat with spoon until batter is smooth.

Gradually add enough remaining flour to make a soft dough that leaves the sides of the bowl.

Turn out on floured surface and knead until smooth and satiny, about 8 to 10 minutes.

Place dough in lightly greased bowl; turn over to grease top. Cover and let rise in warm place until doubled, about 1 hour.

Roll dough ¼" thick on floured surface. Cut with floured 3" round cookie cutter. Place on floured waxed paper. Cover and let rise until doubled, about 45 minutes.

Fry a few doughnuts at a time in hot cooking oil (365°) until golden brown, turning once. Drain on paper towels. Roll doughnuts in sugar. Makes 3½ dozen.

PUFFY POTATO DOUGHNUTS

Unglazed doughnuts can be frozen. Reheat in foil in oven

2 c. milk
½ c. butter or regular
   margarine
1 c. sugar
1 tblsp. salt
1 pkg. active dry yeast
1 tsp. sugar
¼ c. lukewarm water
1 tsp. baking powder

½ tsp. baking soda
1 c. unseasoned mashed
   potatoes
3 egg yolks
8 c. sifted flour
Cooking oil
Vanilla Glaze (recipe
   follows)

Scald milk. Stir in butter, 1 c. sugar and salt. Cool to lukewarm.

Sprinkle yeast and 1 tsp. sugar on lukewarm water; stir to dissolve. Add yeast, baking powder, baking soda, mashed potatoes, egg yolks and 2 c. flour to milk mixture. Beat with electric mixer at medium speed until smooth, about 2 minutes, scraping bowl occasionally. Or beat with spoon until batter is smooth.

Gradually add remaining flour, blending well. (Dough will be soft.) Place in lightly greased bowl; turn dough over to grease top. Cover and let rise in warm place until doubled, about 2 hours.

Roll out dough ¼″ thick on floured surface. Cut with floured doughnut cutter. Place on floured waxed paper. Cover and let rise until doubled, about 1 hour.

Fry a few doughnuts at a time in hot cooking oil (350°) until golden brown, turning once. Drain on paper towels. Coat warm doughnuts with Vanilla Glaze. Place on cooling rack to dry. Makes 3½ dozen.

Vanilla Glaze: Combine 1 lb. box confectioners sugar, ½ c. soft butter or regular margarine, 7 tblsp. milk or light cream and 2½ tsp. vanilla. Beat until smooth.

BEST-EVER DOUGHNUTS

A Missouri Ribbon-winner for 60 years sent this in

4¼ c. sifted flour
4 tsp. baking powder
1¼ tsp. ground nutmeg
½ tsp. salt
2 eggs
1 c. sugar

2 tblsp. melted butter or
   regular margarine
1 c. milk
1 tsp. vanilla
Cooking oil
Sugar

Sift together flour, baking powder, nutmeg and salt.

Beat together eggs and 1 c. sugar until light. Add butter, milk and vanilla. Add dry ingredients all at once, stirring just until smooth. (Dough is very soft.)

Knead dough lightly on floured surface. Roll out dough ⅜″ thick. Cut with floured doughnut cutter.

Fry a few doughnuts at a time in hot cooking oil (370°) until golden brown, turning once. Drain on paper towels. Roll doughnuts in sugar. Makes 2 dozen.

SPICY DOUGHNUTS

Awarded first place in yeast doughnuts in a Missouri fair

3½ c. sifted flour
2 tsp. baking powder
2 tsp. ground cinnamon
1 tsp. baking soda
½ tsp. salt
¼ tsp. ground cloves
¼ tsp. ground nutmeg
¼ tsp. ground mace
4 egg yolks

1 c. sugar
2 tblsp. soft butter or regular
   margarine
¾ c. buttermilk
1 tsp. rum extract
Cooking oil
1 c. sugar
½ tsp. ground cinnamon

Sift together flour, baking powder, 2 tsp. cinnamon, baking soda, salt, cloves, nutmeg and mace.

Beat together egg yolks and 1 c. sugar until light. Add butter, buttermilk and rum extract. Add dry ingredients all at once, stirring just until smooth. (Dough is very soft.) Knead dough lightly on floured surface. Cover and chill at least 1 hour.

Roll out dough ⅜" thick on floured surface. Cut with floured doughnut cutter.

Fry a few doughnuts at a time in hot cooking oil (375°) until golden brown, turning once. Drain on paper towels. Roll doughnuts in combined 1 c. sugar and ½ tsp. cinnamon. Makes 14 doughuts.

TOP WINNERS . . .
TENDER-CRUMBED COFFEE CAKES

"Just took a coffee cake out of the oven and plugged in the percolator—come on over for a coffee break," is a familiar neighborly phone invitation in farm kitchens. When your neighbors sample these prize-winning tender-crumbed coffee cakes, we predict that you will collect compliments and requests for the recipe.

Featuring both yeast and quick coffee cakes, this section will satisfy even the most discriminating sweet tooth. Fair judges placed a satiny Blue or in some cases the distinguished Purple Ribbon beside every one of these beauties.

Sugar-crusted Rhubarb Squares took a Purple at the Nebraska State Fair and doubles nicely as a spring dessert.

The recipe for Refrigerated Cinnamon Coffee Cake makes three cakes from one batch. Topped with sparkling honey glaze and a lavish sprinkling of slivered almonds, this is a handsome coffee cake. In fact, the state fair winner from Kansas confessed that she's lost track of the number of ribbons she has won—both Blues and Purples—over the many years she has entered this in fairs.

You'll love the old-fashioned Fruit-studded Sour Cream Kuchen with bright fruit peeking through the custard filling. We made a peach, a cherry and an apricot kuchen, all superb. This is an heirloom three-generation recipe and a many-time fair winner from Montana.

SUGAR-CRUSTED RHUBARB SQUARES

Also good served with coffee or tea for a break

2½ c. sifted flour
1 tsp. baking soda
1 tsp. salt
1½ c. brown sugar, firmly
   packed
1 egg, beaten
⅔ c. cooking oil
1 c. sour milk

1 tsp. vanilla
1½ c. finely diced fresh
   rhubarb
½ c. chopped walnuts
½ c. sugar
1 tblsp. melted butter or
   regular margarine
½ tsp. ground cinnamon

Sift together flour, baking soda and salt into bowl. Mix in brown sugar.

Combine egg, oil, sour milk and vanilla. Add to dry ingredients, blending well. Stir in rhubarb and walnuts. Spread batter in greased 9″ square baking pan.

Combine sugar, butter and cinnamon; mix well. Sprinkle over batter.

Bake in 325° oven 55 minutes or until done. Cut in squares and serve warm or cold. Makes 9 servings.

REFRIGERATED CINNAMON COFFEE CAKE

This recipe makes three large coffee cakes

2 pkgs. active dry yeast
2½ c. lukewarm water
¾ c. shortening
¾ c. sugar
2½ tsp. salt
2 tsp. almond extract
2 eggs
8 c. sifted flour

Melted butter or regular
   margarine
½ c. sugar
1 tsp. ground cinnamon
Honey Topping (recipe
   follows)
Slivered almonds

Sprinkle yeast on lukewarm water; stir to dissolve. Stir in shortening, ¾ c. sugar, salt, almond extract, eggs and 4 c. flour. Beat with electric mixer at medium speed until smooth, about 2

PINEAPPLE CARROT CAKE

A nine-year-old girl won a top prize with this cake recipe

2 c. sifted flour	1¼ c. cooking oil
1 tsp. baking soda	4 eggs
1 tsp. ground cinnamon	1 tsp. vanilla
½ tsp. ground nutmeg	½ c. chopped walnuts
¼ tsp. ground allspice	1 tsp. flour
¼ tsp. ground cloves	1½ c. grated peeled carrots
¼ tsp. salt	1 (8¼ oz.) can crushed
2 c. sugar	pineapple, drained

Sift together 2 c. flour, baking soda, cinnamon, nutmeg, all-spice, cloves and salt.

Beat together sugar and oil until well blended. Add eggs, one at a time, beating well after each addition. Add vanilla.

Gradually add dry ingredients, beating well after each addition. Combine walnuts and 1 tsp. flour. Stir in walnuts, carrots and pineapple. Pour batter into greased and floured 9″ tube pan.

Bake in 350° oven 1 hour or until cake tests done. Cool in pan on rack 10 minutes. Remove from pan; cool on rack. Makes 12 servings.

GOOD SNACKING CAKES

"Come on over for coffee and a snack." "Hey, Mom, is there anything to eat?" "My committee's coming over this evening—will you have any of this good cake left?"

All these cakes are just right for all kinds of snacks from morning coffee breaks to after-dinner meetings. Expect them to ask for seconds when you bring on the Banana Streusel Cake with its crunchy topping that marbles down through the cake. A Blue and Purple Ribbon winner, Coconut Snack Cake, disappeared like lightning when we served it in our FARM JOURNAL Countryside Test Kitchens.

Children love to find good cupcakes in their lunch boxes.

Chunky Chocolate Cupcakes frosted with Creamy Orange Frosting would be a perfect "trick or treat" at Halloween. A fair winner from Virginia has shared her recipe for Best-ever Chocolate Cupcakes with friends for over 50 years—"My family says they're the best cupcakes they have ever tasted."

BANANA STREUSEL CAKE

Won a Blue Ribbon in a Pennsylvania fair . . . delicious

¾ c. sifted flour	1 c. sifted flour
½ c. sugar	1½ tsp. baking powder
½ c. butter or regular	½ tsp. baking soda
margarine	½ tsp. salt
¼ c. sugar	½ tsp. ground cinnamon
2 eggs	⅔ c. mashed bananas
1 tsp. vanilla	⅓ c. buttermilk

Combine ¾ c. flour and ½ c. sugar in bowl. Cut in butter with pastry blender or two knives until mixture is crumbly. Reserve ½ c. crumbs.

Add ¼ c. sugar, eggs and vanilla to remaining crumb mixture. Beat until smooth.

Sift together 1 c. flour, baking powder, baking soda, salt, and cinnamon. Add dry ingredients alternately with combined bananas and buttermilk, beating well after each addition. Spread batter in greased 10" pie plate. Sprinkle with reserved ½ c. crumbs.

Bake in 375° oven 35 minutes or until cake tests done. Cool in pan on rack. Makes 8 servings.

COCONUT SNACK CAKE

So good! This cake was given a Purple Ribbon in Nebraska

2 c. sifted flour
1 tsp. baking soda
1 tsp. ground cinnamon
½ tsp. salt
⅔ c. shortening
1 c. brown sugar, firmly
  packed
2 eggs

1 tsp. vanilla
1 c. buttermilk
1 c. flaked coconut
1 c. sugar
1 tsp. ground cinnamon
½ tsp. ground nutmeg
¼ c. light cream

Sift together flour, baking soda, cinnamon and salt.

Cream together shortening and brown sugar until light and fluffy. Beat in eggs, one at a time, beating well after each addition. Beat in vanilla.

Add dry ingredients alternately with buttermilk, beating well after each addition. Spread in greased 13×9×2″ cake pan.

Combine coconut, sugar, cinnamon, nutmeg and light cream. Sprinkle over top of batter.

Bake in 350° oven 35 minutes or until cake tests done. Cool in pan on rack. Makes 16 servings.

SPONGE CAKE SQUARES

Delicious served warm for brunch or a coffee break

1½ c. sifted flour
1½ tsp. baking powder
¼ tsp. salt
3 eggs
1½ c. sugar
1 tsp. vanilla

¾ c. milk, scalded
½ c. melted butter or
  regular margarine
Confectioners sugar
Ground cinnamon

Sift together flour, baking powder and salt.

Beat eggs thoroughly. Gradually beat in sugar, beating at high speed until thick and light. Add vanilla. Beat in hot milk. Using low speed on mixer, beat in dry ingredients, mixing well. Pour batter into greased and floured 13×9×2″ baking pan.

Bake in 350° oven 40 minutes or until cake tests done. Remove cake from oven; slowly pour melted butter over top. Sprinkle with confectioners sugar, then cinnamon. Cool in pan on rack. Cut in squares to serve. Makes 12 servings.

CINNAMON APPLE SQUARES

Good dessert choice for a field lunch or snack for the crew

2 c. sifted flour
1 tsp. baking soda
1 tsp. ground cinnamon
½ tsp. salt
1 c. cooking oil
1¾ c. sugar

4 eggs
1 tsp. vanilla
2 c. chopped, pared apples
½ c. chopped walnuts
Vanilla Glaze (recipe
  follows)

Sift together flour, baking soda, cinnamon and salt.

Beat together oil, sugar, eggs and vanilla (about 3 minutes).

Add dry ingredients, beating well after each addition. Stir in apples and walnuts. Pour batter into greased 15½×10½×1" jelly roll pan.

Bake in 350° oven 40 minutes or until cake tests done. Cool in pan on rack.

Spread with Vanilla Glaze. Makes 24 servings.

Vanilla Glaze: Combine 1½ c. sifted confectioners sugar, 2 tblsp. soft butter or regular margarine and 5 tblsp. water. Beat until smooth.

CHUNKY CHOCOLATE CUPCAKES

Won a Purple Ribbon in the 4-H Foods and Nutrition Division

1 c. sifted flour
1 c. sugar
1½ tsp. baking powder
½ tsp. salt
2 eggs
¼ c. cooking oil

1 tsp. vanilla
¼ c. milk
1½ oz. unsweetened
  chocolate, chopped
Creamy Orange Frosting
  (recipe follows)

Sift together flour, sugar, baking powder and salt into bowl.

Combine eggs, oil, vanilla and milk in small bowl. Beat well.

Combine egg mixture with dry ingredients; beat until blended. Stir in chocolate. Spoon batter into paper-lined 2½" muffin-pan cups, filling two-thirds full.

Bake in 400° oven 20 to 25 minutes or until cupcakes test done. Remove from pans; cool on racks.

Frost with Creamy Orange Frosting. Makes 12 cupcakes.

Creamy Orange Frosting: Combine 2½ c. sifted confectioners sugar, 3 tblsp. soft butter or regular margarine, 1 tsp. grated orange rind and 2 tblsp. orange juice. Beat until smooth.

BEST-EVER CHOCOLATE CUPCAKES

A Virginia woman has baked these cupcakes for over 50 years

1½ c. sifted flour	1½ c. sugar
½ c. cocoa	2 eggs
1 tsp. baking soda	1 tsp. vanilla
¼ tsp. salt	½ c. buttermilk
½ c. butter or regular margarine	½ c. hot water

Sift together flour, cocoa, baking soda and salt.

Cream together butter and sugar until light and fluffy. Add eggs, one at a time, beating well after each addition. Beat in vanilla. Add dry ingredients alternately with buttermilk and water, beating well after each addition. Spoon batter into paper-lined 3" muffin-pan cups, filling one-third full.

Bake in 375° oven 20 minutes or until cupcakes test done. Remove from pans; cool on racks. Frost with your favorite chocolate frosting if you wish. Makes 24 cupcakes.

CHOCOLATE CHIP CUPCAKES

Pack these special cupcakes in your children's lunch

2 c. sifted cake flour	2 eggs
3 tsp. baking powder	1½ tsp. vanilla
¾ tsp. salt	⅔ c. milk
½ c. shortening	1 (6 oz. pkg.) semi-sweet
1 c. sugar	chocolate pieces

Sift together cake flour, baking powder and salt.

Cream together shortening and sugar until light and fluffy. Add eggs, one at a time, beating well after each addition. Beat in vanilla. Add dry ingredients alternately with milk, beating well after each addition. Stir in chocolate pieces. Spoon batter into paper-lined 2½″ muffin-pan cups, filling two-thirds full.

Bake in 350° oven 20 minutes or until cupcakes test done. Remove from pans; cool on racks. Makes 26 cupcakes.

RAISIN SURPRISE CAKE

An exceptionally good white cake with raisin filling

3 c. sifted cake flour	1 c. ice water
2 tsp. baking powder	4 egg whites
¼ tsp. salt	½ c. sugar
½ c. butter or regular	Raisin Topping (recipe
margarine	follows)
1½ c. sugar	Fluffy White Frosting
3 tblsp. hot water	(recipe follows)
1 tsp. vanilla	

Sift together cake flour, baking powder and salt.

Cream together butter and 1½ c. sugar until light and fluffy. Add 3 tblsp. hot water and vanilla; beat well.

Add dry ingredients alternately with 1 c. ice water, beating well after each addition.

Beat egg whites until foamy. Gradually add ½ c. sugar beating until stiff peaks form. Fold into batter. Pour batter into greased 13×9×2″ cake pan.

Bake in 350° oven 35 minutes or until cake tests done. Cool in pan on rack.

Spread evenly with Raisin Topping. Carefully spread with Fluffy White Frosting. Makes 16 servings.

Raisin Topping: Combine ¾ c. sugar, 2 tblsp. flour, 1 c. raisins, 2 egg yolks, beaten and 1 c. light cream in small saucepan. Cook over medium heat, stirring constantly, until mixture thickens. Remove from heat; stir in 1 tsp. vanilla and 2 tblsp. butter or regular margarine. Cool well.

Fluffy White Frosting: Combine 1 egg white, ¾ c. sugar, ⅛ tsp. cream of tartar and 3 tblsp. water in top of a double boiler. Place over boiling water and beat with electric mixer at high speed until mixture stands in stiff peaks (about 4 minutes). Remove from heat.

CHOICE CHOCOLATE COLLECTION

This section contains some of the most luscious chocolate cakes in the country. Surprise the men in your family with these dark beauties. Start with Daddy's Chocolate Cake, a 3-time Blue Ribbon winner from California that's rich and easy to make, or the Chocolate Fudge Cake that tastes like an ultra-rich brownie. A field crew gave Moist Chocolate Cake Supreme their "most favorite cake" vote. A delightfully different cake made with thick golden honey, Blue Ribbon Honey Fudge Cake, wins a Blue Ribbon every year it is entered in a Minnesota fair —the rich Caramel Pecan Topping makes this heavenly eating!

DADDY'S CHOCOLATE CAKE

A moist chocolate cake that is so easy to make. Keeps well

2½ c. sifted flour	⅔ c. shortening
1½ c. sugar	2 eggs
½ c. cocoa	1 tsp. vanilla
2 tsp. baking soda	1 c. buttermilk
1 tsp. salt	½ c. water

Sift together flour, sugar, cocoa, baking soda and salt into bowl. Add shortening, eggs, vanilla, buttermilk and water. Beat at medium speed 3 minutes until batter is smooth. Pour into greased and floured 13×9×2″ baking pan.

Bake in 350° oven 35 to 40 minutes or until cake tests done. Cool in pan on rack.

Frost with your favorite chocolate frosting. Makes 16 servings.

CHOCOLATE FUDGE CAKE

This rich cake tastes like a brownie, a tester commented

1 c. sifted flour	4 eggs
1 tsp. baking powder	1 tsp. vanilla
½ c. butter or regular margarine	1 (1 lb.) can chocolate-flavored syrup
1 c. sugar	1 c. chopped walnuts

Sift together flour and baking powder.

Cream together butter and sugar until light and fluffy. Add eggs, one at a time, beating well after each addition. Beat in vanilla.

Add dry ingredients alternately with chocolate-flavored syrup, beating well after each addition. Stir in walnuts. Pour batter into greased and floured 9″ tube pan.

Bake in 350° oven 65 minutes or until cake tests done. Cool in pan on rack 15 minutes. Remove from pan; cool on rack.

If you wish, spread cake with whipped cream and sprinkle with cinnamon. Makes 12 servings.

MOIST CHOCOLATE CAKE SUPREME

Chocolate fans will ask for seconds of this lovely cake

2 c. sugar	2 tsp. baking soda
1 c. cocoa	2 c. warm water
¼ tsp. salt	2¼ c. sifted flour
1 c. cooking oil	Chocolate Satin Frosting
2 eggs	(recipe follows)
1 tsp. vanilla	

Combine sugar, cocoa, salt and oil in bowl; beat until well blended. Add eggs, one at a time, beating well after each addition. Beat in vanilla.

Combine baking soda and water. Add flour to cocoa mixture alternately with soda mixture, beating well after each addition. Pour batter into greased and floured 13×9×2" baking pan.

Bake in 350° oven 45 minutes or until cake tests done. Cool in pan on rack 15 minutes. Remove from pan; cool on rack.

Frost with Chocolate Satin Frosting. Makes 16 servings.

Chocolate Satin Frosting: Combine 3 tblsp. butter or regular margarine and ⅓ c. milk in 2-qt. saucepan. Heat until butter melts. Remove from heat. Sift together 3 c. sifted confectioners sugar and ½ c. cocoa. Stir into hot mixture; beat until smooth. Beat in 1 tsp. vanilla. Spread quickly on cooled cake.

BLUE RIBBON HONEY FUDGE CAKE

This winner has been made over and over by a Minnesota woman

½ c. butter or regular margarine	1 tsp. baking soda
¼ c. sugar	2 tblsp. boiling water
¾ c. honey	3 egg whites
⅛ tsp. salt	¾ c. sugar
½ c. cocoa	Caramel Pecan Topping (recipe follows)
⅓ c. cold water	Chocolate Glaze (recipe follows)
2½ c. sifted cake flour	
1 c. cold water	

Cream together butter, ¼ c. sugar, honey and salt until light and fluffy.

Combine cocoa and ⅓ c. water. Add to creamed mixture, blending well. Add cake flour alternately with 1 c. water, beating well after each addition.

Combine baking soda and 2 tblsp. water. Stir into batter.

Beat egg whites until frothy. Gradually beat in ¾ c. sugar. Fold into batter. Pour batter into greased and floured 13×9×2" baking pan.

Bake in 350° oven 50 minutes or until cake tests done. Cool in pan on rack.

Spread cake with Caramel Pecan Topping. Then spread with Chocolate Glaze. Makes 16 servings.

Caramel Pecan Topping: Combine ⅔ c. brown sugar, firmly packed, 1½ tsp. flour, 2 egg yolks, ⅔ c. milk and 1 tblsp. butter or regular margarine in heavy 2-qt. saucepan. Cook over medium heat, stirring occasionally, until thick (about 15 minutes). Stir in ½ c. chopped pecans. Cool.

Chocolate Glaze: Combine 1 (1 oz.) square unsweetened chocolate, chopped, 1 c. sugar, ¼ c. butter or regular margarine, ⅓ c. milk and ¼ tsp. salt in heavy 2-qt. saucepan. Cook over medium heat, stirring constantly, until mixture boils 1 minute. Remove from heat. Stir in ½ tsp. vanilla. Immediately pour mixture evenly over Caramel Pecan Topping. Work quickly as glaze thickens rapidly.

CHOCOLATE CINNAMON CAKE

An Ohio homemaker added cinnamon to make this different

3 c. sifted cake flour	2¼ c. sugar
½ c. cocoa	2 eggs
2 tsp. baking soda	1 tsp. vanilla
1½ tsp. ground cinnamon	2 c. buttermilk
1 tsp. salt	Creamy Chocolate Frosting
1 c. butter or regular margarine	(recipe follows)

Sift together cake flour, cocoa, baking soda, cinnamon and salt.

Cream together butter and sugar until light and fluffy. Add eggs, one at a time, beating well after each addition. Beat in vanilla.

Add dry ingredients alternately with buttermilk, beating well after each addition. Pour batter into 2 greased and floured 9" square cake pans.

Bake in 350° oven 45 minutes or until cakes test done. Cool in pans on racks 10 minutes. Remove from pans; cool on racks.

Spread the top of one layer with Creamy Chocolate Frosting. Place other layer on top. Frost sides and top of cake with remaining frosting. Makes 12 servings.

Creamy Chocolate Frosting: Cream together 1 (8 oz.) pkg. cream cheese, softened and ⅓ c. soft butter or regular margarine. Sift together 6 c. sifted confectioners sugar and 1 c. cocoa. Add to creamed mixture alternately with ½ c. light cream, blending well after each addition.

DEVIL'S FOOD LAYER CAKE

A family favorite that's been served on many occasions

1 c. sugar	¼ tsp. salt
¾ c. cocoa	¾ c. butter or regular
1 egg, slightly beaten	margarine
1 c. milk	1 c. sugar
2 c. sifted cake flour	2 eggs
1 tsp. baking soda	½ c. milk

Sift together 1 c. sugar and cocoa into heavy 2-qt. saucepan. Stir in 1 egg. Gradually stir in 1 c. milk. Cook over medium heat, stirring constantly, until mixture coats a spoon. Remove from heat; cool completely.

Sift together cake flour, baking soda and salt.

Cream together butter and 1 c. sugar until light and fluffy. Add 2 eggs, one at a time, beating well after each addition. Beat in cooled chocolate mixture.

Add dry ingredients alternately with ½ c. milk, beating well after each addition. Pour batter into 2 greased and floured 9" round cake pans.

Bake in 350° oven 25 minutes or until cakes test done. Cool in pans on racks 10 minutes. Remove from pans; cool on racks. Frost with your favorite frosting. Makes 12 servings.

CHOCOLATE FUDGE SQUARES

These cake squares are especially nice for packed lunches

2 c. sifted flour	4 tblsp. cocoa
2 c. sugar	1 c. cold water
1 tsp. baking soda	2 eggs
1 tsp. ground cinnamon	2 tsp. vanilla
¼ tsp. salt	½ c. buttermilk
½ c. butter or regular margarine	Chocolate Walnut Icing (recipe follows)

Sift together flour, sugar, baking soda, cinnamon and salt into bowl.

Combine butter, cocoa and water in 2-qt. saucepan. Bring to a boil, stirring occasionally. Remove from heat. Pour over flour mixture; mix well. Add eggs, vanilla and buttermilk; beat well. Pour into well-greased 15½ ×10½ ×1″ jelly roll pan.

Bake in 400° oven 20 minutes or until cake tests done. Cool in pan on rack.

Spread with Chocolate Walnut Icing. Makes 15 servings.

Chocolate Walnut Icing: Combine ½ c. butter or regular margarine, 4 tblsp. cocoa and ⅓ c. milk in heavy 2-qt. saucepan. Cook over medium heat, stirring occasionally, until mixture boils. Remove from heat. Stir in 1 (1 lb.) box confectioners sugar, 1 c. chopped walnuts and 1 tsp. vanilla. Beat until smooth. Quickly spread over top of cake.

POTPOURRI OF SPICE CAKES

Many of these spicy country fair winners are the kind of cake that men really go for—good hearty down-to-earth eating. The Fresh Apple Cake is studded with apples—rich, moist and delicious. Cut in squares, served warm with a generous pour of hot lemon sauce, it's a perfect supper finale on a blustery night. Spicy Applesauce Cake, chock-full of raisins, pecans and applesauce would be a perfect midafternoon snack. Great cake to serve guests on a fall day—three-layer Sweet Potato Surprise Cake made from grated raw sweet potatoes—good for you as well as good eating!

FRESH APPLE CAKE

This moist, spicy cake is chock-full of chopped apples

1 c. sifted flour	2 eggs
1 tsp. baking soda	1 tsp. vanilla
1 tsp. ground cinnamon	2½ c. finely chopped, pared
1 tsp. salt	apples
1 c. sugar	1 c. chopped walnuts
½ c. shortening	1 tblsp. flour

Sift together 1 c. flour, baking soda, cinnamon and salt.

Cream together sugar and shortening until light and fluffy. Beat in eggs, one at a time, beating well after each addition. Add vanilla. Add dry ingredients, beating well after each addition. Stir in apples. Combine walnuts and 1 tblsp. flour. Stir into batter. Pour into greased and floured 9″ square baking pan.

Bake in 350° oven 50 minutes or until cake tests done. Cool in pan on rack. If desired, serve cake squares with lemon sauce. Makes 9 servings.

SPICY APPLESAUCE CAKE

An old-fashioned cake that is sure to please your family

1½ c. sifted flour	1 c. sugar
1 tsp. baking soda	2 eggs
1 tsp. ground cinnamon	1 c. applesauce
1 tsp. salt	1 c. raisins
¼ tsp. ground cloves	1 c. chopped pecans
½ c. shortening	1 tblsp. flour

Sift together 1½ c. flour, baking soda, cinnamon, salt and cloves.

Cream together shortening and sugar until light and fluffy. Add eggs, one at a time, beating well after each addition.

Add dry ingredients alternately with applesauce, beating well after each addition. Combine raisins, pecans and 1 tblsp. flour. Stir into batter. Pour batter into greased 9″ square baking pan.

Bake in 350° oven 55 minutes or until cake tests done. Cool in pan on rack. Makes 9 servings.

TWO-LAYER APPLESAUCE CAKE

A great choice for a snack after a brisk autumn hike

4 c. sifted flour	**2 c. sugar**
2 tblsp. cocoa	**3 c. unsweetened applesauce,**
4 tsp. baking soda	**heated**
2 tsp. cinnamon	**½ c. raisins**
1¼ tsp. salt	**½ c. chopped walnuts**
½ tsp. ground nutmeg	**Creamy Butterscotch**
½ tsp. ground cloves	**Frosting (recipe follows)**
1 c. cooking oil	

Sift together flour, cocoa, baking soda, cinnamon, salt, nutmeg and cloves.

Beat together oil and sugar until well blended. Add hot applesauce, beating well.

Gradually add dry ingredients, beating well after each addition. Stir in raisins and walnuts; mix well. Pour batter into 2 greased and floured 9″ square baking pans.

Bake in 400° oven 15 minutes. Reduce heat to 375° and bake 15 minutes or until cakes test done. Cool in pans on racks 5 minutes. Remove from pans; cool on racks.

Spread the top of one layer with Creamy Butterscotch Frosting. Place second layer on top. Frost sides and top of cake with frosting. Makes 12 servings.

Creamy Butterscotch Frosting: Melt ½ c. butter or regular margarine in saucepan over low heat. Stir in 1 c. dark brown sugar, firmly packed and ¼ tsp. salt. Bring mixture to a boil over medium heat; boil 2 minutes, stirring constantly. Remove from heat. Stir in ¼ c. milk. Return to heat; bring to a full boil. Remove from heat; cool to lukewarm. Add 2 c. sifted confectioners sugar; beat until smooth. If frosting becomes too thick, stir in a little more milk.

SWEET POTATO SURPRISE CAKE

This three-layer beauty is sure to win applause

2½ c. sifted cake flour	4 eggs, separated
3 tsp. baking powder	1½ tsp. vanilla
1½ tsp. ground cinnamon	4 tblsp. hot water
1½ tsp. ground nutmeg	1½ c. grated, raw sweet
½ tsp. salt	potatoes
1½ c. cooking oil	1 c. chopped walnuts
2 c. sugar	

Sift together flour, baking powder, cinnamon, nutmeg and salt.

Combine oil and sugar; beat well. Add egg yolks and vanilla; beat until smooth.

Add dry ingredients alternately with hot water, beating well after each addition. Stir in sweet potatoes and walnuts.

Beat egg whites until stiff, but not dry. Fold into batter. Pour batter into 3 greased 8″ round cake pans.

Bake in 350° oven 30 minutes or until cakes test done. Cool in pans on racks 10 minutes. Remove from pans; cool on racks.

Frost with your favorite butter icing. Makes 12 servings.

HARVEST DREAM SPICE CAKE

This cake is subtly flavored with a combination of spices

2½ c. sifted cake flour	¾ c. shortening
3½ tsp. baking powder	1⅔ c. brown sugar, firmly
1 tsp. salt	packed
½ tsp. ground cinnamon	3 eggs
¼ tsp. ground nutmeg	1 tsp. vanilla
¼ tsp. ground allspice	1 c. milk

Sift together cake flour, baking powder, salt, cinnamon, nutmeg and allspice.

Cream together shortening and brown sugar until light and fluffy. Blend in eggs, one at a time, beating well after each addition. Beat in vanilla.

Add dry ingredients alternately with milk, beating well after each addition. Pour batter into 2 greased and waxed-paper-lined 9" round cake pans.

Bake in 350° oven 40 minutes or until cakes test done. Cool in pans on racks 10 minutes. Remove from pans; cool on racks. Makes 12 servings.

SHENANDOAH VALLEY APPLE CAKE

The scrumptious topping makes this a ribbon winner

1 c. cooking oil	1 tsp. baking soda
2 c. sugar	3 c. diced, pared apples
3 eggs	1 c. chopped walnuts
1¼ tsp. vanilla	1 tblsp. flour
2 c. sifted flour	Caramel Topping (recipe
1 tsp. salt	follows)

Beat together oil, sugar, eggs and vanilla (about 3 minutes).

Sift together 2 c. flour, salt and baking soda.

Add dry ingredients, beating well after each addition. Stir in apples.

Combine walnuts and 1 tblsp. flour; stir into batter. Pour into greased and floured 13×9×2" baking pan.

Baking in 350° oven 1 hour or until cake tests done. Cool in pan on rack.

Spread with Caramel Topping. Makes 16 servings.

Caramel Topping: Combine ½ c. butter or regular margarine, 1 c. brown sugar, firmly packed and ¼ c. milk. Bring to a boil and boil 3 minutes. Remove from heat; spread at once over top of cake.

Four superlative baked goodies from fairs: *Golden Carrot Cookies* (page 176), *Golden Crunch Coffee Cake* (page 61), feathery light *Cottage Cheese Rolls* (page 27) and sugar-coated, *Best-ever Doughnuts* (page 56).

Tried and true Blue Ribbon winners in the Bread Division. We feature here on the upper left: *Cornmeal Surprise Muffins* (page 52); center: *Golden Sesame Braid* (page 16) and *Honey Swirl Coffee Cake* (page 62).

Four columns of doughnuts with different coatings. All are made from the versatile *Puffy Potato Doughnuts* recipe (page 55). They are luscious whether served sugared, glazed, dusted with confectioners sugar or plain.

Moist *Perfect Spice Cake* (page 89) is frosted with swirls of tawny beige frosting. This is handsome enough to serve as a birthday cake or for the holidays. Decorate with candied cherries and walnuts for Thanksgiving.

OATMEAL SPICE CAKE

A great choice to serve for field lunches or picnics

1 c. quick-cooking oats	1 tsp. ground cinnamon
½ c. butter or regular margarine, cut in small pieces	½ tsp. ground allspice
	½ tsp. ground nutmeg
	½ tsp. salt
1½ c. boiling water	2 eggs
1½ c. sifted flour	1 c. brown sugar, firmly packed
1 c. sugar	
1 tsp. baking soda	Coconut Topping (recipe follows)

Combine oats, butter and boiling water in bowl. Cool.

Sift together flour, sugar, baking soda, cinnamon, allspice, nutmeg and salt.

Add eggs to oat mixture; beat well. Add dry ingredients and brown sugar to oat mixture; beat at medium speed 2 minutes. Pour batter into greased 13×9×2" baking pan.

Bake in 350° oven 30 to 35 minutes or until cake tests done.

Spread with Coconut Topping. Place under the broiler for 2 to 3 minutes or until golden brown. Cool in pan on rack. Makes 16 servings.

Coconut Topping: Combine 1 c. coconut, 1 c. brown sugar, firmly packed, 1 c. chopped walnuts and ½ c. milk; mix well.

PERFECT SPICE CAKE

Wreathe with walnut halves for a handsome garnish

2¼ c. sifted cake flour	1 c. sugar
1 tsp. baking powder	¾ c. dark brown sugar, firmly packed
1 tsp. salt	
1 tsp. ground cinnamon	3 eggs
¾ tsp. baking soda	1 tsp. vanilla
¼ tsp. ground cloves	1 c. sour milk
1/16 tsp. pepper	Sea Foam Frosting (recipe follows)
¾ c. shortening	

Sift together cake flour, baking powder, salt, cinnamon, baking soda, cloves and pepper.

Cream together shortening and sugars until light and fluffy. Add eggs, one at a time, beating well after each addition. Beat in vanilla.

Add dry ingredients alternately with sour milk, beating well after each addition. Pour batter into 3 greased and floured 9" round cake pans.

Bake in 350° oven 25 minutes or until cakes test done. Cool in pans on racks 10 minutes. Remove from pans; cool on racks.

Spread the top of one layer with Sea Foam Frosting. Place second layer on top; spread with frosting. Place third layer on top. Frost sides and top of cake with frosting. Makes 12 servings.

Sea Foam Frosting: Combine 2 egg whites, 1½ c. brown sugar, firmly packed, ⅓ c. water and 1 tsp. vanilla in double boiler top. Place over simmering water. Cook for 7 minutes, beating with an electric mixer until soft peaks form. Remove from heat.

SWEET POTATO CAKE

Decorate top of frosted cake with ring of chopped walnuts

3½ c. sifted flour	1 c. cooking oil
2 tsp. baking soda	2¾ c. sugar
1 tsp. ground cloves	2 eggs
1 tsp. ground cinnamon	1 c. mashed, cooked sweet
1 tsp. ground nutmeg	potatoes (2 medium)
¾ tsp. baking powder	1 c. water
¾ tsp. salt	

Sift together flour, baking soda, cloves, cinnamon, nutmeg, baking powder and salt.

Combine oil, sugar and eggs. Beat until smooth. Beat in sweet potatoes.

Add dry ingredients alternately with water, beating well after each addition. Pour batter into 3 greased and waxed-paper-lined 9" round cake pans.

Bake in 350° oven 40 minutes or until cakes test done. Cool in pans on racks 10 minutes. Remove from pans; cool on racks.

Frost with your favorite butter cream frosting. Makes 12 servings.

GREAT GINGERBREADS

Just about everyone loves gingerbread—whether it's served warm from the oven slathered with softened butter, or topped with a dollop of soft whipped cream or a scoop of vanilla ice cream.

We have a variety of winners at fairs: a three-generation heirloom Maple-flavored Gingerbread, delightful mingling of maple and molasses; a Crumb-topped Gingerbread that has been an old faithful for 43 years, and Old-fashioned Gingerbread that dates back to the First World War.

A Blue Ribbon winner told us that her Aunt Dorothy's Gingerbread was always made by her mother and taken to school parties. Now she bakes a big pan for her children's school functions and always comes home with an empty pan—not even a crumb left!

MAPLE-FLAVORED GINGERBREAD

This many-ribbon-winner is so good topped with whipped cream

2½ c. sifted flour	½ c. shortening
1½ tsp. baking soda	½ c. sugar
1 tsp. ground cinnamon	1 egg
1 tsp. ground ginger	½ c. molasses
½ tsp. ground cloves	½ c. maple-flavored syrup
½ tsp. salt	1 c. hot water

Sift together flour, baking soda, cinnamon, ginger, cloves and salt.

Cream together shortening and sugar until light and fluffy. Add egg; beat well. Gradually beat in molasses and maple-flavored syrup.

Add dry ingredients alternately with water, beating well after each addition. Pour batter into greased 13×9×2″ baking pan.

Bake in 350° oven 30 minutes or until cake tests done. Cool in pan on rack. Makes 16 servings.

CRUMB-TOPPED GINGERBREAD

This golden-colored gingerbread is one family's favorite

2 c. sifted flour	1 egg
1 c. sugar	2 tblsp. molasses
1½ tsp. ground ginger	1 tsp. baking soda
1 tsp. ground cinnamon	½ tsp. salt
½ c. shortening	1 c. sour milk

Sift together flour, sugar, ginger and cinnamon into bowl. Cut in shortening with pastry blender or two knives until mixture is crumbly. Remove ½ c. crumbs; set aside.

Stir egg, molasses, baking soda, salt and sour milk into remaining crumb mixture; blending well. Pour batter into greased 8″ square pan. Sprinkle with reserved ½ c. crumbs.

Bake in 350° oven 45 minutes or until cake tests done. Cool in pan on rack. Makes 9 servings.

OLD-FASHIONED GINGERBREAD

"Deep, dark gingerbread like Grandmother used to make"

2½ c. sifted flour	½ c. shortening
1½ tsp. baking soda	½ c. sugar
1 tsp. ground ginger	1 egg
1 tsp. ground cinnamon	1 c. dark molasses
½ tsp. salt	½ c. hot water

Sift together flour, baking soda, ginger, cinnamon and salt.

Cream together shortening and sugar until light and fluffy. Add egg; beat well. Beat in molasses.

Add dry ingredients alternately with water, beating well after each addition. Pour batter into greased 9″ square baking pan.

Bake in 350° oven 45 minutes or until cake tests done. Cool in pan on rack. Makes 9 servings.

AUNT DOROTHY'S GINGERBREAD

A good choice when it's your turn to serve refreshments

3 c. sifted flour
1 tsp. ground ginger
⅔ c. butter or regular
   margarine
1 c. sugar

3 eggs
1 c. molasses
1½ tsp. baking soda
1 c. boiling water

Sift together flour and ginger.

Cream together butter and sugar until light and fluffy. Add eggs, one at a time, beating well after each addition. Beat in molasses.

Dissolve baking soda in water. Add dry ingredients alternately with baking soda mixture, beating well after each addition. Pour batter into greased 13×9×2″ baking pan.

Bake in 350° oven 35 minutes or until cake tests done. Cool in pan on rack. Makes 16 servings.

BASIC SPICY GINGERBREAD

Top with vanilla ice cream and sprinkle with cinnamon

1 c. sifted flour
1 tsp. baking soda
½ tsp. salt
½ tsp. ground cinnamon
½ tsp. ground nutmeg
¼ tsp. ground cloves

½ c. molasses
1 egg, beaten
¼ c. sugar
¼ c. melted shortening
½ c. hot water

Sift together flour, baking soda, salt, cinnamon, nutmeg and cloves.

Combine molasses, egg and sugar; beat well.

Add dry ingredients to molasses mixture, mix well.

Blend in shortening, then hot water. Pour batter into greased and floured 8″ square baking pan.

Bake in 350° oven 30 to 35 minutes or until cake tests done. Cool in pan on rack. Makes 9 servings.

THE ELEGANTS . . . ANGEL AND SPONGE CAKES

Tall and regal, delicate as a feather—all these cakes are multi-ribbon winners; after testing, we know why.

You'll love the glorious golden sponge cakes—some are plain with just a sifting of confectioners sugar and others are fancy with fillings and glazes.

The ethereal angel foods are high, light and tender. Planning a party? Why not whip up the Brown Sugar Angel Food Cake—it *is* heavenly.

BROWN SUGAR ANGEL FOOD CAKE

Delicate brown sugar flavor makes this angel food different

1¼ c. sifted cake flour	1 tsp. salt
1 c. brown sugar, firmly packed	1 c. brown sugar, firmly packed
1½ c. egg whites (10 to 12)	2 tsp. vanilla
1½ tsp. cream of tartar	Confectioners sugar

Combine cake flour and 1 c. brown sugar.

Beat egg whites, cream of tartar and salt until foamy. Gradually add 1 c. brown sugar, 1 tblsp. at a time, beating at high speed until stiff glossy peaks form. Blend in vanilla.

Add flour mixture in 4 parts, folding about 15 strokes after each addition. Spoon batter into ungreased 10″ tube pan. Pull metal spatula through batter once to break large air bubbles.

Bake in 350° oven 45 to 50 minutes or until cake tests done. Invert tube pan on funnel or bottle to cool. When completely cooled, remove from pan. Dust with sifted confectioners sugar. Makes 12 servings.

BEST ANGEL FOOD CAKE

An elegant cake to serve at showers and other parties

1 c. sifted cake flour	¾ tsp. salt
¾ c. sugar	¾ c. sugar
1¾ c. egg whites (about 12)	1 tsp. vanilla
1½ tsp. cream of tartar	¼ tsp. almond extract

Sift together cake flour and ¾ c. sugar.

Beat egg whites, cream of tartar and salt until foamy. Add ¾ c. sugar, 1 tblsp. at a time, beating at high speed until stiff glossy peaks form. Blend in vanilla and almond extract.

Add flour mixture in 4 parts, folding about 15 strokes after each addition. Spoon batter into ungreased 10″ tube pan. Pull metal spatula through batter once to break large air bubbles.

Bake in 375° oven 35 minutes or until cake tests done. Invert tube pan on funnel or bottle to cool. When completely cooled, remove from pan. Makes 12 servings.

NEVER-FAIL ANGEL FOOD

Lovely served with sliced fresh peaches or strawberries

1 c. sifted cake flour	¼ tsp. salt
½ c. sugar	1 c. sugar
13 egg whites	1 tsp. vanilla
2 tsp. cream of tartar	

Sift together cake flour and ½ c. sugar.

Beat egg whites, cream of tartar and salt until foamy. Add 1 c. sugar, 1 tblsp. at a time, beating at high speed until stiff glossy peaks form. Blend in vanilla.

Add flour mixture in 4 parts, folding about 15 strokes after each addition. Spoon batter into ungreased 10″ tube pan. Pull metal spatula through batter once to break large air bubbles.

Bake in 375° oven 35 minutes or until cake tests done. Invert tube pan on funnel or bottle to cool. When completely cooled, remove from pan. Makes 12 servings.

LEMON SUNSHINE CAKE

We suggest a lemon filling to enhance this fair winner

8 eggs, separated
½ c. sugar
2 tblsp. cold water
½ tsp. vanilla
½ tsp. almond extract
½ tsp. lemon extract
1¼ c. sifted flour

½ tsp. cream of tartar
½ tsp. salt
1 c. sugar
Lemon Custard Filling
  (recipe follows)
Confectioners sugar

Combine egg yolks, ½ c. sugar, water, vanilla, almond and lemon extracts. Beat at high speed until thick and lemon-colored (about 5 minutes). Stir in flour all at once.

Beat egg whites, cream of tartar and salt at high speed until foamy. Gradually beat in 1 c. sugar, beating until stiff moist peaks form. Pull metal spatula through batter once to break large air bubbles.

Gradually fold egg yolk mixture into egg whites. Pour batter into ungreased 10″ tube pan.

Bake in 325° oven 60 to 65 minutes or until cake tests done. Invert tube pan on funnel or bottle to cool. When completely cooled, remove from pan.

Cut cake into 3 layers. Spread with Lemon Custard Filling. Dust with confectioners sugar. Makes 12 servings.

Lemon Custard Filling: Prepare 1 (2 oz.) envelope whipped topping mix according to package directions. Prepare 1 (3¼ oz.) pkg. instant lemon pudding according to package directions, but using 1 c. milk. Fold pudding into prepared topping mix.

ORANGE SPONGE CAKE

Makes a perfect base for fresh strawberries and cream

6 eggs, separated
1 c. sugar
1 tblsp. grated orange rind
½ c. orange juice

1⅓ c. sifted flour
1 tsp. cream of tartar
¼ tsp. salt
½ c. sugar

Combine egg yolks, 1 c. sugar, orange rind and orange juice. Beat at high speed until thick and lemon-colored, about 5 minutes. Stir in flour, a little at a time, mixing well.

Beat egg whites, cream of tartar and salt at high speed until frothy. Gradually add ½ c. sugar, beating until stiff glossy peaks form.

Gradually fold egg yolk mixture into egg whites. Pour batter into ungreased 10″ tube pan. Pull metal spatula through batter once to break large air bubbles.

Bake in 325° oven 55 minutes or until cake tests done. Invert tube pan on funnel or bottle to cool. When completely cooled, remove from pan. Makes 12 servings.

GOLDEN SPONGE CAKE

Try our decorating suggestion for this tried and true winner

12 eggs, separated	1 pt. heavy cream, whipped
½ tsp. salt	and sweetened
1 tsp. cream of tartar	Assorted canned fruits,
1⅓ c. sugar	drained
1 tsp. vanilla	Fresh mint leaves (optional)
1⅓ c. sifted cake flour	

Beat egg whites at high speed until frothy. Add salt and cream of tartar; beat until stiff peaks form. Gradually add sugar, beating until soft glossy peaks form. Blend in vanilla.

Sift cake flour over egg white mixture in 4 equal parts; fold in carefully.

Beat egg yolks until thick and lemon-colored (about 5 minutes). Fold egg yolks into egg white mixture. Pour batter into ungreased 10″ tube pan. Pull metal spatula through batter once to break large air bubbles.

Bake in 325° oven 1 hour 15 minutes or until cake tests done. Invert tube pan on funnel or bottle to cool. When completely cooled, remove from pan.

Swirl whipped cream over surface of cake. Decorate top with fruits and mint leaves. Makes 12 servings.

GLORIOUS SPONGE CAKE

Winner of a satin Purple Ribbon at the Kansas State Fair

6 eggs, separated	1¼ c. sifted cake flour
½ c. sugar	½ tsp. cream of tartar
¼ c. cold water	¼ tsp. salt
1 tsp. lemon extract	½ c. sugar
1 tsp. grated lemon rind	

Combine egg yolks, ½ c. sugar, water, lemon extract and lemon rind. Beat at high speed until thick and lemon-colored (about 5 minutes). Stir in cake flour all at once.

Beat egg whites, cream of tartar and salt at high speed until frothy. Gradually beat in ½ c. sugar, beating until stiff glossy peaks form.

Gradually fold egg yolk mixture into egg whites. Pour batter into ungreased 9″ tube pan. Pull metal spatula through batter once to break large air bubbles.

Bake in 325° oven 1 hour or until cake tests done. Invert tube pan on funnel or bottle to cool. When completely cooled, remove from pan. Makes 12 servings.

YELLOW SPONGE CAKE

Serve thin slices of this cake with sweetened fresh fruit

1½ c. sifted cake flour	1 tsp. vanilla
½ tsp. baking powder	½ tsp. lemon extract
6 eggs, separated	¾ tsp. cream of tartar
½ c. cold water	¼ tsp. salt
1½ c. sugar	

Sift together cake flour and baking powder.

Combine egg yolks, water, sugar, vanilla and lemon extract. Beat at high speed until very thick and lemon-colored (about 5 minutes). Stir in dry ingredients all at once.

Beat egg whites at high speed until frothy. Add cream of tartar and salt; continue beating until stiff but not dry peaks form.

Gradually fold egg yolk mixture into egg whites. Pour batter into ungreased 9" tube pan. Pull metal spatula through batter once to break large air bubbles.

Bake in 325° oven 1 hour or until cake tests done. Invert tube pan on funnel or bottle to cool. When completely cooled, remove from pan. Makes 12 servings.

CHAMPION SPONGE CAKE

This cake is a lovely addition to any buffet or luncheon

1¼ c. sifted flour	½ c. sugar
1 c. sugar	¼ c. water
½ tsp. baking powder	1 tsp. vanilla
½ tsp. salt	Pineapple Frosting (recipe
6 eggs, separated	follows)
1 tsp. cream of tartar	

Sift together flour, 1 c. sugar, baking powder and salt.

Beat egg whites at high speed until frothy. Add cream of tartar. Gradually add ½ c. sugar, beating until stiff but not dry peaks form.

Combine egg yolks, water, vanilla and dry ingredients. Beat at medium high speed until thick and lemon-colored (about 4 minutes).

Gradually fold egg yolk mixture into egg whites. Pour batter into ungreased 10" tube pan.

Bake in 350° oven 45 minutes or until cake tests done. Invert tube pan on funnel or bottle to cool. When completely cooled, remove from pan.

Frost sides and top with Pineapple Frosting. Makes 12 servings.

Pineapple Frosting: Cream together ¼ c. butter or regular margarine and ¼ c. shortening. Gradually add 3 c. sifted confectioners sugar; beat until light and fluffy. Stir in 1 (8½ oz.) can drained crushed pineapple, ⅛ tsp. salt, ¼ tsp. vanilla and ½ tsp. grated lemon rind.

PRIZED CHIFFONS

These velvety-crumbed chiffon cakes deserve every ribbon they have won. Blue Ribbon Peppermint Chiffon, delicately pink, with a faint sting of mint, frosted with puffy swirls of icing and wreathed with crushed peppermint candy is a beauty. "Tastes like banana ice cream," commented one of our staff testers when she sampled the Banana Custard Chiffon Cake. We served each slice with a small scoop of banana ice cream and a ladle of crushed fresh strawberries. Try the other chiffons —each one is a delightful eating experience.

BLUE RIBBON PEPPERMINT CHIFFON

A Grand Champion winner in the 4-H Chiffon Cake Division

2½ c. sifted cake flour	½ c. cold water
1½ c. sugar	1½ tsp. peppermint extract
3 tsp. baking powder	½ tsp. vanilla
1 tsp. salt	½ tsp. cream of tartar
½ c. cooking oil	15 drops red food color
7 eggs, separated	

Sift together cake flour, sugar, baking powder and salt into bowl. Make a well in the center. Add oil, egg yolks, water, peppermint extract and vanilla. Beat with electric mixer at low speed 1 minute. (Or beat with spoon until smooth.)

Beat egg whites and cream of tartar until stiff peaks form. Gradually pour egg yolk mixture over whites, fold just until blended. Pour ⅓ of batter into another bowl. Tint pink with red food color.

Alternate large spoonfuls of pink and plain batter in ungreased 10″ tube pan. Run a spatula through batter to create a swirl effect.

Bake in 325° oven 55 minutes; increase heat to 350° and bake 15 minutes more or until cake tests done. Invert tube pan on funnel or bottle to cool. When completely cooled, remove from pan. Makes 12 servings.

BANANA CUSTARD CHIFFON CAKE

Extra good when topped with swirls of whipped cream

2¼ c. sifted cake flour	¾ c. mashed bananas
1½ c. sugar	(2 medium)
3 tsp. baking powder	1 tblsp. lemon juice
1 tsp. salt	1 tsp. vanilla
½ c. cooking oil	1 c. egg whites (7 or 8)
5 egg yolks	½ tsp. cream of tartar

Sift together cake flour, sugar, baking powder and salt into bowl. Make a well in the center. Add oil, egg yolks, bananas, lemon juice and vanilla. Beat with electric mixer at low speed 1 minute. (Or beat with spoon until smooth.)

Beat egg whites and cream of tartar until stiff peaks form. Gradually pour egg yolk mixture over whites, folding just until blended. Pour batter into ungreased 10″ tube pan. Cut through batter with metal spatula.

Bake in 325° oven 50 to 60 minutes or until cake tests done. Invert tube pan on funnel or bottle to cool. When completely cooled, remove from pan. Makes 12 servings.

SPICY CHIFFON CAKE

This cake is the winner of several ribbons and trophies

2 c. sifted flour	½ tsp. ground allspice
1½ c. sugar	½ tsp. ground cloves
3 tsp. baking powder	½ c. cooking oil
1 tsp. salt	7 eggs, separated
1 tsp. ground cinnamon	¾ c. cold water
½ tsp. ground nutmeg	½ tsp. cream of tartar

Sift together flour, sugar, baking powder, salt, cinnamon, nutmeg, allspice and cloves into bowl. Make a well in the center. Add oil, egg yolks and water. Beat with electric mixer at low speed 1 minute. (Or beat with spoon until smooth.)

Beat egg whites and cream of tartar until stiff peaks form.

Gradually pour egg yolk mixture over whites, folding just until blended. Pour into ungreased 10″ tube pan. Cut through batter with spatula.

Bake in 325° oven 55 minutes, then increase heat to 350° and bake 10 to 15 minutes more or until cake tests done. Invert tube pan on funnel or bottle to cool. When completely cooled, remove from pan. Frost as desired. Makes 12 servings.

MAPLE CHIFFON CAKE

Judges at an Ohio fair awarded a Blue Ribbon to this cake

2¼ c. sifted flour	8 eggs, separated
1½ c. sugar	¾ c. cold water
3 tsp. baking powder	2 tsp. maple flavoring
1 tsp. salt	½ tsp. cream of tartar
½ c. cooking oil	Vanilla ice cream

Sift together flour, sugar, baking powder and salt into bowl. Make a well in the center. Add oil, egg yolks, water and maple flavoring. Beat with electric mixer at low speed 1 minute. (Or beat with spoon until smooth.)

Beat egg whites and cream of tartar until stiff peaks form. Gradually pour egg yolk mixture over whites, folding just until blended. Pour batter into ungreased 10″ tube pan. Cut through batter with spatula.

Bake in 350° oven 1 hour 10 minutes or until cake tests done. Invert cake on funnel or bottle to cool. When completely cooled, remove from pan.

Top cake slices with vanilla ice cream. Makes 12 servings.

ORANGE CHIFFON CAKE

Frost with 7-minute frosting for a lovely birthday cake

2 c. sifted flour	8 eggs, separated
1½ c. sugar	¾ c. cold water
3 tsp. baking powder	2 tblsp. grated orange rind
1 tsp. salt	½ tsp. cream of tartar
½ c. cooking oil	

Sift together flour, sugar, baking powder and salt into bowl. Make a well in the center. Add oil, egg yolks, water and orange rind. Beat with electric mixer at low speed 1 minute. (Or beat with spoon until smooth.)

Beat egg whites and cream of tartar until stiff peaks form. Gradually pour egg yolk mixture over whites, folding just until blended. Pour batter into ungreased 10" tube pan. Cut through batter with spatula.

Bake in 325° oven 1 hour 5 minutes or until cake tests done. Invert tube pan on funnel or bottle to cool. When completely cooled, remove from pan. Makes 12 servings.

PRAISE-WINNING POUND CAKES

Rich and buttery—good solid eating down to the last crumb describes this medley of pound cakes. Serve Spiced-up Apple Cider Pound Cake on a crisp fall day with mugs of cocoa at a Halloween party. Topped with a shiny caramel glaze this is an "original" recipe from a Texas winner—it captured the Grand Champion Purple Ribbon over 160 cakes. Then there's an heirloom: Grandmother's Buttermilk Pound Cake laced with faint almond flavor and drizzled with an almond-scented glaze. For a spring party, present the Million Dollar Pound Cake with its tangy lemon glaze on your prettiest plate. You will collect heaps of compliments from all these popular pound cakes.

SPICED-UP APPLE CIDER POUND CAKE

A Texas woman developed this recipe; her husband named it

3 c. flour	½ c. shortening
½ tsp. salt	3 c. sugar
½ tsp. baking powder	6 eggs
¾ tsp. ground cinnamon	1 tsp. vanilla
½ tsp. ground allspice	1 c. apple cider
½ tsp. ground nutmeg	Caramel Icing (recipe
¼ tsp. ground cloves	follows)
1 c. butter	

Sift together flour, salt, baking powder, cinnamon, allspice, nutmeg and cloves.

Cream together butter, shortening and sugar until light and fluffy, about 10 minutes. Add eggs, one at a time, beating 1½ minutes after each addition. Add vanilla.

Add dry ingredients alternately with apple cider, beating well after each addition. Pour batter into greased and floured 10" tube pan.

Bake in 325° oven 1 hour 30 minutes or until cake tests done. Cool in pan on rack 15 minutes. Remove from pan; cool on rack. When slightly cooled, pour Caramel Icing evenly over cake. Makes 12 servings.

Caramel Icing: Combine ½ c. sugar, ¼ tsp. baking soda, ¼ c. butter or regular margarine, ¼ c. buttermilk, ½ tblsp. light corn syrup and ¼ tsp. vanilla in small saucepan. Bring to a rolling boil. Boil 10 minutes, stirring occasionally.

GRANDMOTHER'S BUTTERMILK POUND CAKE

An heirloom recipe that won a Blue Ribbon in California

3 c. sifted flour	**2 tsp. vanilla**
¼ tsp. baking soda	**¼ tsp. almond extract**
½ c. butter	**1 c. buttermilk**
2 c. sugar	**Almond Glaze (recipe**
4 eggs	**follows)**

Sift together flour and baking soda.

Cream together butter and sugar until light and fluffy. Add eggs, one at a time, beating well after each addition. Add vanilla and almond extract. (Total beating time: 10 minutes.)

Add dry ingredients alternately with buttermilk, beating well after each addition. Pour batter into well-greased 9" tube pan.

Bake in 350° oven about 1 hour 25 minutes or until cake tests done. Cool in pan on rack 15 minutes. Remove from pan; cool on rack.

Spoon Almond Glaze over top of cake. Let some of glaze drip down sides. Makes 12 servings.

Almond Glaze: Combine 1½ c. sifted confectioners sugar, 2 to 3 tblsp. milk and ½ tsp. almond extract. Stir until smooth.

MILLION DOLLAR POUND CAKE

The hint of lemon makes this pound cake special

3 c. sifted flour
½ tsp. salt
¼ tsp. baking soda
1 c. shortening
3 c. sugar
6 eggs

2 tsp. lemon extract
1 tsp. vanilla
1 c. buttermilk
Lemon Glaze (recipe
   follows)

Sift together flour, salt and baking soda.

Cream together shortening and sugar until light and fluffy. Add eggs, one at a time, beating well after each addition. Add lemon extract and vanilla. (Total beating time: 10 minutes.)

Add dry ingredients alternately with buttermilk, beating well after each addition. Pour batter into well-greased and floured 10″ fluted tube pan.

Bake in 325° oven 1 hour 20 minutes or until cake tests done. Cool in pan on rack for 15 minutes. Remove from pan; cool on rack.

Spoon Lemon Glaze over top of cake. Let some of glaze drip down sides. Makes 12 servings.

Lemon Glaze: Combine 1½ c. sifted confectioners sugar, ½ tsp. grated lemon rind and 3 tblsp. lemon juice. Stir until smooth.

DELUXE POUND CAKE

Excellent, fine-textured pound cake with buttery flavor

2 c. butter (1 lb.)
3 c. sugar
6 eggs
1½ tsp. vanilla

4 c. sifted cake flour
⅔ c. milk
Confectioners sugar

Cream together butter and sugar until light and fluffy. Add eggs, one at a time, beating well after each addition. Add vanilla. (Total beating time: 10 minutes.)

Add cake flour alternately with milk, beating well after each addition. Pour batter into well-greased 10″ fluted tube pan.

Bake in 350° oven 1 hour 30 minutes or until cake tests done. Cool in pan on rack 15 minutes. Remove from pan; cool on rack. Dust with confectioners sugar. Makes 12 servings.

Note: Cake is best if covered and allowed to stand for 24 hours before serving.

POUND CAKE DELIGHT

A tender-crumbed pound cake that won a Texas Blue Ribbon

3 c. sifted flour	**6 eggs**
1 tsp. baking powder	**1½ tsp. rum extract**
½ tsp. salt	**1 tsp. lemon extract**
1 c. butter	**1 c. milk**
½ c. shortening	**Tangy Lemon Glaze (recipe**
3 c. sugar	**follows)**

Sift together flour, baking powder and salt.

Cream together butter, shortening and sugar until light and fluffy. Add eggs, one at a time, beating well after each addition. Add rum and lemon extract. (Total beating time: 10 minutes.)

Add dry ingredients alternately with milk, beating well after each addition. Pour batter into greased and floured 10″ tube pan.

Bake in 325° oven 1 hour 30 minutes or until cake tests done. Cool in pan on rack 15 minutes. Remove from pan; cool on rack.

Prepare Tangy Lemon Glaze. Place cake bottom side up on serving plate. Punch holes in top of cake with meat fork. Spoon glaze over cake. Makes 12 servings.

Tangy Lemon Glaze: Combine ½ c. sugar and ¼ c. water in small saucepan. Bring mixture to a boil, stirring constantly. Boil 2 minutes. Stir in ¼ tsp. lemon extract.

"COMPANY'S COMING" CAKES

Every guest will ask for the recipe when you serve any one of these cakes. "This Toasted Pecan Cake is scrumptious and that's putting it mildly," the proud winner of two Blue Ribbons from Oklahoma told us as we sampled the cake and heartily agreed.

A many-ribboned winner, Poppy Seed Cake is a square beauty with a luscious Butterscotch Filling and a Chocolate Icing. This farm cook from Wisconsin wins the Blue whether she uses the filling and chocolate icing or simply frosts with a basic butter cream.

When the bounty of summer fruit is at its peak, you simply must impress your guests with the Tropical Butter Cake—it's a beauty! Baked in a ring mold, the center is filled with assorted fresh fruits of the season and then topped with soft puffs of whipped cream.

TOASTED PECAN CAKE

If you really like pecans, use them on top for decoration

1⅓ c. coarsely chopped pecans	1⅓ c. sugar
3 tblsp. butter or regular margarine	3 eggs
2 c. sifted flour	1½ tsp. vanilla
1½ tsp. baking powder	⅔ c. milk
¼ tsp. salt	Butter Cream Frosting (recipe follows)
⅔ c. butter or regular margarine	

Combine pecans and 3 tblsp. butter in a shallow baking pan. Toast pecans in 350° oven 15 minutes, stirring occasionally. Cool.

Sift together flour, baking powder and salt.

Cream together butter and sugar until light and fluffy. Add

eggs, one at a time, beating well after each addition. Beat in vanilla.

Add dry ingredients alternately with milk, beating well after each addition. Stir in 1 c. of the toasted pecans; reserve remaining ⅓ c. for frosting. Pour batter into 2 greased and floured 8″ round cake pans.

Bake in 350° oven 30 to 35 minutes or until cakes test done. Cool in pans on racks 10 minutes. Remove from pans; cool on racks.

Spread the top of one layer with Butter Cream Frosting. Place second layer on top. Frost sides and top of cake with frosting. Decorate cake with remaining ⅓ c. pecans. Makes 12 servings.

Butter Cream Frosting: Combine 3 tblsp. soft butter or regular margarine, 3 c. sifted confectioners sugar, 3 tblsp. light cream or milk and 1 tsp. vanilla; stir until smooth. Add more light cream, if necessary, to make frosting of spreading consistency.

POPPY SEED CAKE

Always a favorite, this poppy seed cake has a luscious filling

2¼ c. sifted flour	1 tsp. vanilla
1½ c. sugar	4 egg whites
4 tsp. baking powder	Butterscotch Filling (recipe
1 tsp. salt	follows)
½ c. poppy seeds	Chocolate Icing (recipe
½ c. shortening	follows)
1 c. milk	

Sift together flour, sugar, baking powder and salt into bowl. Add poppy seeds, shortening and milk. Beat with electric mixer at high speed 2 minutes. Add vanilla and egg whites; beat 2 more minutes. Pour into 2 greased and floured 9″ square pans.

Bake in 350° oven 30 minutes or until cakes test done. Cool in pans on racks 10 minutes. Remove from pans; cool on racks.

Spread the top of one layer with Butterscotch Filling. Place other layer on top. Frost sides and top of cake with Chocolate Icing. Makes 12 servings.

Butterscotch Filling: Combine ¾ c. brown sugar, firmly packed, 2 tblsp. cornstarch and ½ c. chopped walnuts in heavy 2-qt. saucepan. Gradually stir in 1¼ c. scalded milk. Cook over medium heat, stirring constantly, until mixture thickens (about 8 minutes). Beat 4 egg yolks slightly. Add some of the hot mixture into the egg yolks. Then stir the egg yolk mixture into remaining hot mixture. Cook, stirring constantly, about 1 minute. Remove from heat. Stir in 1 tsp. vanilla. Cool well.

Chocolate Icing: Combine 1 (3 oz.) pkg. softened cream cheese, 1 (1 oz.) square unsweetened chocolate, melted, 2½ c. sifted confectioners sugar, 1 tblsp. milk and 1 tsp. vanilla. Mix until smooth, adding more milk if necessary.

TROPICAL BUTTER CAKE

Welcome summer's bounty with this cake filled with fruits

1½ c. sifted flour	1 tsp. grated orange rind
1½ tsp. baking powder	⅓ c. milk
¼ tsp. salt	2 tblsp. orange juice
½ c. butter	Confectioners sugar
¾ c. sugar	Fresh fruit*
1 egg	½ c. heavy cream, whipped
½ tsp. vanilla	

Sift together flour, baking powder and salt.

Cream together butter and sugar until light and fluffy. Add egg, vanilla and orange rind; beat well.

Add dry ingredients alternately with milk and orange juice, beating well after each addition. Pour into buttered and floured 5-cup ring mold.

Bake in 350° oven 30 to 35 minutes or until cake tests done. Cool in mold on rack 5 minutes. Remove from mold; cool on rack.

Dust top of cake with confectioners sugar. Fill center with fruit. Top with whipped cream. Makes 8 servings.

* Any type of fresh fruit can be used, such as: sliced peaches, pears, strawberries, raspberries, blueberries and oranges. If you wish, add a little sugar to fruit. One fruit can be served or a combination of several. Canned, drained fruits are also good.

BASIC WHITE LAYER CAKE

This cake is also good with a creamy chocolate frosting

2¼ c. sifted flour	½ tsp. baking soda
1 tsp. baking powder	1 tblsp. water
½ c. shortening	1 c. buttermilk
1 c. sugar	4 egg whites
1 tsp. vanilla	½ c. sugar

Sift together flour and baking powder.

Cream together shortening and 1 c. sugar until light and fluffy. Add vanilla.

Dissolve baking soda in water. Combine with buttermilk.

Add dry ingredients alternately with buttermilk mixture, beating well after each addition.

Beat egg whites until foamy. Gradually beat in ½ c. sugar, beating until soft peaks form. Fold into creamed mixture. Pour batter into 3 greased and waxed-paper-lined 8″ round pans.

Bake in 350° oven 30 minutes or until cakes test done. Cool in pans on racks 10 minutes. Remove from pans; cool on racks.

Frost with your favorite white frosting. Makes 12 servings.

FRESH ORANGE LAYER CAKE

Delicate orange layers with creamy nut-studded frosting

2½ c. sifted cake flour	1½ tsp. grated orange rind
1½ c. sugar	½ c. fresh orange juice
2 tsp. baking powder	½ c. milk
1 tsp. salt	2 eggs
¼ tsp. baking soda	Creamy Nut Frosting (recipe
½ c. shortening	follows)

Sift together flour, sugar, baking powder, salt and baking soda into bowl.

Add shortening, orange rind and orange juice; beat with electric mixer at medium speed 2 minutes. Add milk and eggs; beat 2 more minutes. Pour batter into 2 greased 8″ round cake pans.

Bake in 350° oven 30 minutes or until cakes test done. Cool in pans on racks 10 minutes. Remove from pans; cool on racks.

Spread the top of one layer with reserved Creamy Nut Frosting. Place second layer on top. Frost sides and top of cake with remaining Creamy Nut Frosting. Makes 12 servings.

Creamy Nut Frosting: Gradually blend ½ c. milk into 2½ tblsp. cake flour in small saucepan. Cook, stirring constantly, until mixture is a thick paste (about 10 minutes). Cool to lukewarm. Cream together ½ c. butter or regular margarine, ½ c. sugar and ¼ tsp. salt. Add milk mixture; beat until fluffy. Stir in ½ tsp. vanilla and ½ c. coarsely chopped nuts. Reserve ⅓ c. for filling. Add 1 c. sifted confectioners sugar to remainder, blending until smooth.

FLUTED ORANGE CAKE

The secret of this cake is its yummy orange-flavored glaze

2¼ c. sifted flour	4 eggs
1½ c. sugar	1 c. orange juice
3 tsp. baking powder	1 tsp. grated orange rind
1 tsp. salt	Orange Sugar Glaze (recipe
1 (2 oz.) env. whipped	follows)
topping mix	Flaked coconut
⅔ c. shortening	

Sift together flour, sugar, baking powder, salt and whipped topping mix into bowl. Add shortening, eggs, orange juice and orange rind. Blend until dry ingredients are moistened, then beat with electric mixer at medium speed 4 minutes. Spoon batter into greased and floured 10″ fluted tube pan.

Bake in 350° oven 40 minutes or until cake tests done. Cool in pan on rack 15 minutes. Remove from pan; place on rack. Spread while warm with Orange Sugar Glaze; sprinkle with coconut. Makes 12 servings.

Orange Sugar Glaze: Gradually add 1½ c. sifted confectioners sugar to ¼ c. hot orange juice. Add ½ tsp. grated orange rind. Beat until mixture is smooth.

FIRST-PRIZE BANANA CAKE

Glamorous with swirls of frosting and toasted coconut top

2 c. sifted cake flour	1 tsp. vanilla
1 tsp. baking soda	½ c. buttermilk
1 tsp. baking powder	½ c. chopped pecans
½ tsp. salt	1 c. flaked coconut
¾ c. shortening	Pecan Filling (recipe
1½ c. sugar	follows)
2 eggs	Fluffy Frosting (recipe
1 c. mashed bananas	follows)

Sift together cake flour, baking soda, baking powder and salt.

Cream together shortening and sugar until light and fluffy. Add eggs, one at a time, beating well after each addition. Beat in bananas and vanilla; blend well.

Add dry ingredients alternately with buttermilk, beating well after each addition. Stir in pecans. Pour batter into 2 greased and floured 9" round cake pans. Sprinkle top of each with ½ c. coconut.

Bake in 375° oven 25 to 30 minutes or until cakes test done. Cool in pans on racks 10 minutes. Remove from pans; cool on racks.

Place first layer, coconut side down, and spread with Pecan Filling. Top with second layer, coconut side up. Spread with Fluffy Frosting on sides and about 1" around top edge, leaving center unfrosted. Makes 12 servings.

Pecan Filling: Combine ½ c. sugar, 2 tblsp. flour, ½ c. light cream and 2 tblsp. butter or regular margarine in small heavy saucepan. Cook over medium heat, stirring constantly, until thickened. Add ½ c. chopped pecans, ¼ tsp. salt and 1 tsp. vanilla; mix well. Cool well.

Fluffy Frosting: Combine 1 egg white, ¼ c. shortening, ¼ c. butter or regular margarine and 1 tsp. vanilla. Beat until smooth and creamy. Gradually add 2 c. sifted confectioners sugar, beating until light and fluffy.

BUTTERSCOTCH LAYER CAKE

This luscious cake won a Blue in a Michigan county fair

2¼ c. sifted cake flour
1½ tsp. baking powder
1 tsp. salt
½ c. shortening
1½ c. brown sugar, firmly packed

⅔ c. milk
1½ tsp. vanilla
2 eggs
⅓ c. milk
Creamy Butterscotch Frosting (recipe follows)

Sift together cake flour, baking powder and salt into bowl. Add shortening, brown sugar, ⅔ c. milk and vanilla. Beat with electric mixer at medium speed for 2 minutes, scraping bowl occasionally. Add eggs and ⅓ c. milk; beat for 2 more minutes. Pour batter into 2 greased and waxed-paper-lined 9″ round cake pans.

Bake in 350° oven 30 minutes or until cakes test done. Cool in pans on racks 10 minutes. Remove from pans; cool on racks.

Spread the top of one layer with Creamy Butterscotch Frosting. Place second layer on top. Frost sides and top of cake with remaining frosting. Makes 12 servings.

Creamy Butterscotch Frosting: Melt ½ c. butter or regular margarine in small saucepan. Add 1 c. brown sugar, firmly packed. Stir until sugar is dissolved. Remove from heat. Cool slightly. Add ¼ c. milk; beat until smooth. Gradually add 2 c. sifted confectioners sugar, beating well. Blend in 1 tsp. vanilla. Beat until frosting is of spreading consistency.

SPECTACULARS FOR SPECIAL OCCASIONS

Graduation, bridal shower, bon voyage or farewell party coming up? That's when you want to serve something that's a little different and very special—the kind of cake that when you bring it out on your loveliest dish will evoke "Oh, look at that!"

"The very first time I entered my Mile-high Buttermilk Cake it won first prize and was I happy! My mother-in-law gave me the recipe years ago and I make it only for special occasions," a proud winner from Tennessee told us. Chocolate Shadow Cake, a black and white dazzler when cut, makes a two-layer cake look like four. For an elegant ladies' tea, the Raspberry Cream Roll would be a perfect choice.

MILE-HIGH BUTTERMILK CAKE

Everyone on our Test Kitchen staff gave this an "Excellent"

4 c. sifted cake flour	1 tblsp. vanilla
1 tsp. baking soda	2 c. buttermilk
½ tsp. baking powder	6 egg whites
½ tsp. salt	Creamy Vanilla Filling
1 c. butter or regular	(recipe follows)
margarine	Orange Butter Frosting
3 c. sugar	(recipe follows)

Sift together cake flour, baking soda, baking powder and salt.

Cream together butter and sugar until light and fluffy. Beat in vanilla.

Add dry ingredients alternately with buttermilk, beating well after each addition. Add egg whites; beat at medium speed 2 minutes. Pour batter into 3 waxed-paper-lined 9" round cake pans.

Bake in 350° oven 20 minutes; reduce heat to 325° and bake 25 more minutes or until cakes test done. Cool in pans on racks 10 minutes. Remove from pans; cool on racks.

Spread the top of one layer with half of Cream Vanilla Filling. Place second layer on top. Spread with remaining half of filling. Top with third layer. Frost sides and top of cake with Orange Butter Frosting. Makes 12 servings.

Creamy Vanilla Filling: Prepare 1 (3¼ oz.) pkg. vanilla pudding and pie filling according to package directions for pie filling. Cool well.

Orange Butter Frosting: Combine 5 c. sifted confectioners sugar, ½ c. soft butter or regular margarine, ¼ tsp. almond extract and 2 to 3 tblsp. orange juice. Beat until smooth.

RASPBERRY CREAM ROLL

Originally filled with lemon pudding; so good either way

1 c. sifted flour	½ c. water
2 tsp. baking powder	1 tsp. lemon extract
½ tsp. salt	Confectioners sugar
10 egg yolks	Raspberry Cream Filling
1 c. sugar	(recipe follows)

Sift together flour, baking powder and salt.

Combine egg yolks, sugar, water and lemon extract in small bowl. Beat until thick and lemon-colored (about 5 minutes).

Fold in dry ingredients a little at a time. Spread batter into greased and waxed-paper-lined 15½×10½×1″ jelly roll pan.

Bake in 400° oven 20 minutes or until cake tests done. Loosen cake around edges. Turn out on dish towel dusted with sifted confectioners sugar. Trim off browned crust along edges. Roll up, starting at narrow side, rolling towel up with cake. Cool completely.

Unroll cake and spread with Raspberry Cream Filling to within ½″ of edges. Reroll cake, using the towel to help make a tight roll. Place open end down. Refrigerate until serving time. Sprinkle with sifted confectioners sugar. Makes 12 servings.

Raspberry Cream Filling: Whip ½ pt. heavy cream until soft peaks form. Fold in 1 (10 oz.) pkg. frozen raspberries, thawed and well drained.

LEMON CREAM ROLL

Light and tangy cake roll is a real springtime treat

1 c. sifted flour	¼ c. boiling water
½ tsp. cream of tartar	Confectioners sugar
¼ tsp. salt	1 (3¾ oz.) pkg. instant
3 eggs	lemon pudding
1 c. sugar	1 tsp. grated lemon rind
2 tsp. lemon extract	½ c. heavy cream, whipped
¼ tsp. baking soda	

Sift together cake flour, cream of tartar and salt.

Combine eggs, sugar and lemon extract in bowl. Beat until thick and lemon-colored.

Fold dry ingredients into egg mixture.

Dissolve baking soda in boiling water. Blend into batter. Spread batter into greased and waxed-paper-lined 15½ × 10½ - × 1" jelly roll pan.

Bake in 375° oven 12 to 15 minutes or until cake tests done. Loosen cake around edges. Turn out on dish towel dusted with sifted confectioners sugar. Trim off browned crust along edges. Roll up, starting at narrow side, rolling towel up with cake. Cool completely.

Prepare instant lemon pudding according to package directions. Stir in lemon rind.

Unroll cake and spread with 1 c. lemon filling to within ½" of edges. Reroll cake, using the towel to help make a tight roll. Place open end down.

Fold whipped cream into remaining lemon filling. Spread thickly on outside of cake roll. If you wish, decorate with lemon slices and maraschino cherries. Refrigerate until serving time. Leftover filling (if any) may be spooned over cake slices when served. Makes 8 servings.

CHOCOLATE SHADOW CAKE

This white cake looks glamorous with its chocolate stripes

2¼ c. sifted flour	4 egg whites
1½ c. sugar	1 c. finely chopped pecans
4 tsp. baking powder	2 (1 oz.) squares
1 tsp. salt	unsweetened chocolate,
⅔ c. shortening	grated
1¼ c. milk	Dark Chocolate Frosting
1 tsp. vanilla	(recipe follows)

Sift together flour, sugar, baking powder and salt into bowl. Add shortening, milk and vanilla. Beat with electric mixer at medium speed 1½ minutes. Add egg whites; beat for 2 more minutes.

Sprinkle pecans in 2 greased and waxed-paper-lined 9″ round cake pans. Spoon ¼ of batter carefully in each prepared cake pan. Sprinkle each with chocolate. Spoon remaining batter evenly into each pan.

Bake in 350° oven 35 minutes or until cakes test done. Cool in pans on racks 10 minutes. Remove from pans; cool on racks.

Place one layer, nut side up, on plate. Spread with Dark Chocolate Frosting. Place second layer on top, nut side up. Frost sides and top of cake with frosting. Makes 12 servings.

Dark Chocolate Frosting: Combine 4 (1 oz.) squares unsweetened chocolate, ½ c. sugar and ¼ c. water in 2-qt. heavy saucepan. Cook over low heat, stirring constantly, until chocolate melts and mixture is smooth. Remove from heat. Stir in 4 beaten egg yolks; beat well. Cool. Cream together ½ c. shortening, 2 c. sifted confectioners sugar and 1 tsp. vanilla. Slowly add in chocolate mixture, beating well. Blend in 3 tblsp. milk, beating until frosting is of spreading consistency.

MY FAVORITE JELLY ROLL

This Minnesota woman has won several ribbons over the years

¾ c. sifted cake flour
¾ tsp. baking powder
¼ tsp. salt
5 eggs
¾ c. sugar

½ tsp. almond extract
Confectioners sugar
1 c. apricot preserves or any
    other jam or jelly

Sift together cake flour, baking powder and salt.

Combine eggs, sugar and almond extract in bowl. Beat until thick and lemon-colored (about 5 minutes).

Fold dry ingredients into egg mixture. Spread batter in greased and waxed-paper-lined 15½ ×10½ ×1″ jelly roll pan.

Bake in 350° oven 20 minutes or until cake tests done. Loosen cake around edges. Turn out on dish towel dusted with sifted confectioners sugar. Trim off browned crust along edges. Roll up, starting at narrow side, rolling towel up with cake. Cool completely.

Unroll cake and spread with apricot preserves to within ½" of edges. Reroll cake, using the towel to help make a tight roll. Place open end down. Makes 8 servings.

WHITE COCONUT CAKE

This talented Iowa woman enjoys making cakes from scratch

2¼ c. sifted cake flour	1 tsp. vanilla
2¼ tsp. baking powder	1 c. ice water
¼ tsp. salt	4 egg whites
½ c. shortening	½ c. sugar
1 c. sugar	½ c. flaked coconut

Sift together cake flour, baking powder and salt.

Cream together shortening and 1 c. sugar until light and fluffy. Beat in vanilla.

Add dry ingredients alternately with ice water, beating well after each addition.

Beat egg whites until foamy. Gradually add ½ c. sugar, beating until stiff peaks form. Fold into batter. Pour batter into 2 waxed-paper-lined 8" round cake pans.

Bake in 350° oven 30 minutes or until cakes test done. Cool in pans on racks 10 minutes. Remove from pans; cool on racks.

Prepare your favorite fluffy white frosting. Frost cake and garnish with flaked coconut. Makes 12 servings.

MARASCHINO CHERRY CAKE

Tint frosting pink for a special Valentine's Day cake

2¼ c. sifted cake flour	¼ c. maraschino cherry
1½ c. sugar	juice
3½ tsp. baking powder	4 egg whites
1 tsp. salt	18 maraschino cherries,
½ c. shortening	drained and finely
2 tsp. almond extract	chopped
1 tsp. vanilla	½ c. chopped walnuts
¾ c. milk	1 tblsp. flour

Sift together cake flour, sugar, baking powder and salt into mixing bowl. Add shortening, almond extract, vanilla and milk. Beat with electric mixer at high speed 2 minutes. Add maraschino cherry juice and egg whites. Beat at high speed 2 minutes.

Combine cherries, walnuts and flour. Stir into batter. Pour batter into 2 greased and floured 8″ round cake pans.

Bake in 350° oven 35 minutes or until cakes test done. Cool in pans on racks 10 minutes. Remove from pans; cool on racks.

Frost with your favorite fluffy white frosting tinted pink with red food color. Makes 12 servings.

SHOW STOPPERS: DECORATED CAKES

Crowds were always four or five deep around the Decorated Cake Division at the fairs we visited. "Oh, look at that clown! . . . I like the green turtle . . . I think I'll try to make those bells for my New Year's Eve Party"—these were some of the comments we heard.

Homemakers are always eager for new ideas for cake decorating to surprise their family and friends on special occasions. At the fairs we saw many elaborately decorated cakes. Many of these Blue Ribbon winners were almost at a professional level. They had taken beginner's and advanced cake decorating courses and some even conducted demonstration classes of their own. We also saw some winners that were not necessarily elaborate; instead their cakes were perfectly frosted and they had used simple but bright imaginative ideas for decorating. We borrowed some of their ideas and came up with some "conversation piece" cakes for all seasons and occasions. With just a little patience and practice, you will be able to adapt these suggestions and produce a decorated cake that will be the hit of the party.

The children will clap their hands with delight when Tobie the Turtle is brought to the table—especially fun for a little boy's birthday treat. Little girls will love the Fluffy White Coconut Cat all aglow with birthday candles. This is a three-dimensional cat fashioned from two round layers—looks difficult but it is really easy to put together.

For a spring or summer birthday, present a Sweet Violet Cake—it's a cake cut into a violet shape complete with green stems, dainty and delicate.

Watch a little boy's face light up when you sing "Happy Birthday" and bring on his very own Candy-filled Wagon Cake pulled by a giant gingerbread man. The children can dip into the wagon and help themselves to candy before the cake is cut.

The Elegant Easter Egg, pale and pretty with tiny pink flowers, is baked in a melon mold. This would be a pretty cake for an Easter birthday.

After a back-yard barbecue birthday celebration, bring on the Golden Pineapple Cake. It looks like a fresh pineapple and tastes like it too—there's crushed pineapple in the cake batter.

The brightly decorated Grandmother's Patchwork Quilt Cake will delight any age for a birthday celebration.

After you have tried some of these cakes, you'll want to experiment with different decorating tips for flowers and borders and create your own original special-occasion cake.

CANDY-FILLED WAGON CAKE

This clever birthday cake is so easy to decorate

1 (13×9×2″) oblong cake	Assorted candies and
Creamy Butter Frosting	animal cookies
(see Index)	1 large gingerbread man
Yellow food color	Red licorice string
Creamy Chocolate Icing	
(see Index)	

Place cake on large tray or platter.

Tint Creamy Butter Frosting bright yellow. Frost sides and top of cake.

Using tip 21 with Creamy Chocolate Icing, pipe a border around top edge of cake to form sides of wagon. Also pipe another border around bottom of edge of cake.

Two company desserts that will bring rounds of applause. The *Custard Apple Tart* (page 190) looks like it's right out of a French bakery; glazed *Danish Apple Bars* (page 163) like apple pie, but more elegant.

These two prize-winners are perfect to serve on special occasions. On the left: *Golden Sponge Cake* (page 97) is wreathed with colorful fruits and the *Raspberry Cream Roll* (page 115) is lovely dusted with confectioners sugar.

A trio of delicious cakes with creamy frostings. On the left: *First-Prize Banana Cake* (page 112); center: *Two-layer Applesauce Cake* (page 86) and *Champion Sponge Cake* (page 99) swirled with pineapple frosting.

Every bite of this luscious *Apricot Lattice Pie* (page 191) will bring praise from your guests. A delightfully different dessert for your Thanksgiving menu. *Chinese Almond Cookies* (page 145) will sell like wildfire at bazaars.

Pipe *Happy Birthday* with child's name using tip 2 on ⅔ of cake. Arrange assorted candies and animal cookies on remaining ⅓ of cake. Animal cookies can be placed in frosting around sides of wagon, if you wish.

Place gingerbread man in front of wagon. Attach red licorice string to front of wagon and put in hand of gingerbread man. Makes 16 servings.

MOTHER'S DAY BASKET

Surprise your mother with this work of art on her Day

2 (9″) round cake layers	**Creamy Chocolate Icing (see**
Lemon Butter Cream (see	**Index)**
Index)	**Assorted large gumdrops,**
Food colors	**jellied fruit slices and**
	jelly beans

Place 1 cake layer on serving plate.

Tint 2 cups Lemon Butter Cream peach or any desired color. Spread on top of cake layer. Top with remaining cake layer. Frost sides and top of cake.

Using tip 21 with Creamy Chocolate Icing, pipe a basket shape on top of cake about 3″ high and 4″ wide at top tapering to 2″ wide at bottom. Make woven effect, by piping icing in vertical strips about ½″ apart. Then pipe icing in horizontal strips about ½″ apart.

Tint remaining Lemon Butter Cream green. Using tip 96, make a border along bottom edge of cake and then along top edge of cake.

Cut assorted gumdrops and fruit slices into wedges or other shapes to make flowers. Green gumdrops can be cut into stems and leaf shapes. Jelly beans can be used for flower centers. Arrange flowers, stems and leaves above basket in pleasing design. Makes 12 servings.

ELEGANT EASTER EGG

Makes a lovely centerpiece for the Easter dinner table

1 (18½ oz.) pkg. yellow cake mix	Red food color
Creamy Butter Frosting (see Index) 2 recipes	Green food color

Prepare yellow cake mix according to package directions. Pour batter into greased and floured 2-qt. melon mold.

Bake in 350° oven 50 minutes or until cake tests done.

Using 2 cups untinted Creamy Butter Frosting, frost surface of cake.

Tint 1½ cups of Creamy Butter Frosting pale pink. Using tip 64, pipe a border along bottom edge of cake. When piping border, move tip from side to side in a wavy motion.

Pipe another border about 1½″ above first one.

Tint ½ c. Creamy Butter Frosting green. Using tip 4, pipe 2″ long strips, attaching to top border at 1″ intervals to form loops.

Using tip 24 with remaining untinted Creamy Butter Frosting, pipe tiny flowers at each point where loops attach to top border.

Using tip 8 with remaining pink Creamy Butter Frosting, pipe small flowers over surface of egg about ½″ apart.

Using tip 24 with remaining white Creamy Butter Frosting, pipe tiny flowers in center of each pink flower.

Using tip 67 with remaining green Creamy Butter Frosting, pipe 1 or 2 leaves on each pink flower. Makes 12 servings.

MERRY SANTA CAKE

This happy Santa face will delight all your children

1 (18½ oz.) pkg. yellow cake mix	Red glossy decorating gel
	1 black jelly bean
Lemon Butter Cream (see Index)	1 black licorice string
	1 large red gumdrop
Flaked coconut	Red colored sugar

Prepare yellow cake mix according to package directions. Pour batter into 2 greased and floured foil Santa-shaped cake pans.* Bake as directed for layer cake pans.

Place 1 Santa layer on larger serving plate. (Freeze other one for later use. Or if you wish to decorate both at once, double the ingredients listed above.)

Frost sides and top of cake with untinted Lemon Butter Cream.

Arrange coconut over beard and mustache area. Use red glossy decorating gel to fill in hat area. Cut black jelly bean in half and place in position for eyes. Cut black licorice string into short pieces and place in position for eyebrows. Cut large red gumdrop into pieces for both the nose and the mouth and place on face. Sprinkle red colored sugar on cheeks.

Using tip 21 with remaining white Lemon Butter Cream, pipe along edge of hat with two or three wavy lines. Also accent tassel with large puff of frosting. Each cake makes 8 servings.

* Can be purchased in variety stores and supermarkets.

EASY-TO-MAKE CHRISTMAS MOTIF CAKE

By changing the center motif, cake looks different each time

2 (9″) round cake layers	Green food color
Lemon Butter Cream (see Index)	Red glossy decorating gel

Place 1 cake layer on serving plate.

Tint 1½ cups Lemon Butter Cream bright green. Spread on top of cake layer. Top with remaining cake layer. Frost sides and top of cake.

Cut a Christmas motif from a discarded Christmas greeting card, such as: angel, snowman, small child or Santa. Place in center of cake.

Using tip 96 with remaining untinted Lemon Butter Cream, pipe small flowers around edge of Christmas motif.

Using red glossy decorating gel, pipe centers in each small flower.

Press a star or bell-shaped cookie cutter into sides of cake in 5 places. Fill impression made by cutter with small white flowers using tip 96.

Using tip 21 with remaining untinted Lemon Butter Cream, pipe a border around top edge of cake. Makes 12 servings.

DOUBLE BELL SHOWER CAKE

Tint frosting to match dress color of wedding party

1 (18½ oz.) pkg. yellow
    cake mix
Decorating Frosting (see
    Index)

Green food color
Yellow glossy decorating
    gel

Prepare yellow cake mix according to package directions. Pour batter into 2 greased and floured foil bell-shaped cake pans.* Bake as directed for layer cake pans. Or bake in two 9″ round cake pans. When baked, cut round layers into bell shapes.

Arrange bells side by side on large serving tray. Frost sides and top of bells with untinted Decorating Frosting.

Tint 1 cup Decorating Frosting pale green or any other desired color. Using tip 96, pipe small flowers along bottom edge of bells. Then pipe flowers along top edge.

Using tip 3 with white Decorating Frosting, pipe small white centers in each flower.

Using tip 97 and remaining untinted Decorating Frosting, make 6 large roses. Place 3 roses near top of each bell. Make several small buds and place in an attractive design.

Using tip 99 and remaining green Decorating Frosting, pipe leaves among roses where needed.

If you wish, additional roses can be made with remaining untinted Decorating Frosting and placed around bells.

Using yellow glossy decorating gel, pipe *Best Wishes* on bells, one word on each. Makes 16 servings.

Note: This bell cake is also appropriate for a New Year's Eve party.

* Can be purchased in variety stores and supermarkets.

GOLDEN PINEAPPLE CAKE

Serve this cake for a Hawaiian luau or outdoor barbecue

1 (18½ oz.) pkg. yellow cake mix	Decorating Frosting (see Index)
1 (8½ oz.) can crushed pineapple, drained	Food colors Brown licorice strings

Prepare yellow cake mix according to package directions. Stir crushed pineapple into batter. Pour batter into greased and waxed-paper-lined 13×9×2″ baking pan. Bake as directed.

Using a sharp knife, cut cake into shapes for pineapple. Cut a (9×7″) oval for main part of pineapple. From remaining cake, cut 5 pineapple leaf-shaped pieces for leaves. Arrange cut pieces on large foil-covered bread board or cardboard. Use small amounts of Decorating Frosting to "glue" pieces together.

Tint ⅔ of Decorating Frosting gold, using yellow and red food color. Frost sides and top of main part of pineapple. Cut strips of brown licorice strings and lay diagonally on frosted area, about 1½″ apart. Tuck ends of strips into cake. Lay strips of brown licorice in opposite direction, making diamond shapes. Cut small bits of licorice and place in each diamond.

Tint remaining Decorating Frosting green. Frost sides and top of leaves. Makes 16 servings.

JOLLY CIRCUS CLOWN

This clown makes a delightful child's birthday cake

1 (13×9×2″) oblong cake	Assorted large gumdrops
Decorating Frosting (see Index)	Flaked coconut Black licorice string
Food colors	

Using a sharp knife, cut the clown shapes from baked cake. Cut 1 (7½×5½″) oval for body; 2 teardrop shapes (3¾″ long) for shoes; 1 triangle (3½″ high) for hat; 2 (3″) rounds for head and balloon and 3 (1¼″) rounds for hands and top of hat. Arrange cut pieces on large foil-covered bread board or cardboard. Use small amounts of Decorating Frosting to "glue" pieces together.

Tint ⅓ of frosting green for hat and body. Using tip 21, pipe stars close together over surface and sides of body and hat.

Tint ⅓ of frosting pale pink. Spread on hands and face. Decorate face with bits of gumdrops, making mouth, nose and eyes.

Tint ⅙ of frosting as desired to make shoes. (Melted chocolate can be used.)

Tint remaining frosting as desired for balloon. If you wish, sprinkle balloon with colored coconut. Use black licorice string for balloon string. Makes 16 servings.

ANIMAL MERRY-GO-ROUND CAKE

Attractive gumdrop animals on cake appeal to children

2 (9″) round cake layers	**Assorted jellied fruit slices**
Decorating Frosting (see	**Assorted large gumdrops**
Index)	**Toothpicks**
Food color	
6 assorted striped candy	
sticks (6″ long)	

Place 1 cake layer on serving plate.

Tint 3½ c. Decorating Frosting bright yellow. Spread on top of cake layer. Top with remaining cake layer. Frost sides and top of cake.

Tint remaining Decorating Frosting bright green. Using tip 64, pipe a border along bottom edge of cake. When piping border, move tip from side to side in a wavy motion.

Pipe another border along the top edge of cake.

Using tip 21 and remaining green frosting, pipe stripes about ½″ apart between the two borders all around the cake.

Place the 6 candy sticks equally spaced on the top of the cake.

Fashion small birds and animals out of the gumdrops and

jellied fruit slices. For instance, use a jellied fruit slice for a bird's body. Attach two toothpicks for legs and one toothpick for a neck. Cut another fruit slice in half for the head. Two large gumdrops placed with bottoms together secured with a toothpick make a basic animal body. Use your imagination to make the legs and heads of the animals. Place about 4 to 6 animals on top of the cake. Makes 12 servings.

TOBIE THE TURTLE

This easy-to-make birthday cake will please children

1 (13×9×2″) oblong cake	Creamy Chocolate Icing
Creamy Butter Frosting	(see Index)
(see Index)	1 jelly bean
Food color	1 black licorice string

Using a sharp knife, cut the turtle shapes from baked cake. Cut 1 semi-circle from long side of cake (7″ high); 1 tear-drop shape (5½″ long) for head; 2 (4×2¼″) ovals for legs and a (3½″ high) triangle for the tail. Arrange cut pices on large foil-covered bread board or cardboard. Use small amounts of Creamy Butter Frosting to "glue" pieces together.

Tint Creamy Butter Frosting bright green. Frost sides and surface of turtle shell.

Using tip 21 with Creamy Chocolate Icing, pipe lines along edge of turtle shell. If you wish, also pipe wavy lines on shell to add interest. Using tip 21, pipe remaining Creamy Chocolate Icing in either lines or small stars over sides and tops of head, legs and tail.

Use a jelly bean for the eye. Cut a piece of licorice string for the mouth. Makes 12 servings.

GRANDMOTHER'S PATCHWORK QUILT CAKE

A special occasion cake sure to please people of all ages

1 (9″) square cake	Food color
Creamy Butter Frosting (see	Assorted large and small
Index)	gumdrops

Place cake on serving plate.

Frost sides and top of cake with untinted Creamy Butter Frosting.

Tint remaining frosting in desired colors. Using tip 21, with one color, pipe lines vertically and horizontally to make 16 equal-size squares.

Frost alternate squares with various colors.

Cut gumdrops into small flowers and fruits. Place in remaining squares. Use several bright colors to give patchwork effect. Makes 9 servings.

FLUFFY WHITE COCONUT CAT

Surprise a little girl with this cute birthday cake

2 (9″) round cake layers   **Food color**
7-Minute Frosting (see   **Flaked coconut**
  Index)   **Black licorice string**

Using a sharp knife, cut 1 layer in half crosswise. Stand on cut ends, side by side on serving plate or foil-covered board.

Cut 1″ wide strip (7″ long) from around outer edge of other layer for tail. With toothpicks or skewers, secure to back of cat's body.

Cut 2 pieces, 4″ long and 1½″ wide at one end tapering to nothing at other end for paws. Place at front of cat, tapered ends out and slightly apart.

Cut 3″ circle from remaining cake for head. Stand it up on paws, turned slightly to the side. Secure with toothpicks.

Frost cat with 7-Minute Frosting. With spatula, build up extra icing on top of head for ears. Tint a small amount of frosting pale pink and use to frost the inside of the ears.

Tint a small amount of frosting blue. Use to make eyes. Cover entire surface of cat with coconut except for eyes and inside of ears. Cut licorice string in six 3″ strips. Place in position for whiskers, three on each side of face. Makes 12 servings.

WHIMSICAL BUTTERFLY CAKE

A colorful design to brighten any birthday party table

2 (9″) round cake layers	2 black licorice strings
Lemon Butter Cream (see Index)	1 large orange gumdrop
	9 yellow jelly beans
Food color	1 large black gumdrop

Place 1 cake layer on serving plate. Spread with 2½ cups Lemon Butter Cream. Top with second cake layer. Frost sides and top of cake.

Tint remaining Lemon Butter Cream bright aqua; set aside.

Sketch an outline of a butterfly on top of cake. Make body in a teardrop shape (4½″ long and 1½″ wide). Outline with black licorice strings. Cut strips of orange gumdrop and place in horizontal lines across body to make stripes.

Outline 2 large wings (3¼″ long and 2¼″ wide) and 2 smaller wings (3″ long and 1¾″ wide). Spread wing area with aqua frosting. Cut the jelly beans in half. Place 5 in each large wing and 4 in each small wing, cut side down. Cut two (3″) lengths of black licorice strings to make antennae. Cut black gumdrop in half. Place sticky side up in position for head. Position antennae accordingly. Makes 12 servings.

GOLDEN BOOK CAKE

Versatile cake for graduation, confirmation or christening

1 (13×9×2″) oblong cake	Yellow glossy decorating gel
Lemon Butter Cream (see Index)	6 large yellow gumdrops
Food color	3 large green gumdrops

Place cake on foil-covered bread board or cardboard cut to size for book cover with long side of cake parallel to counter top or table edge.

Using a sharp knife, cut a wedge about ½″ deep across center of cake vertically and remove piece of cake.

Cut and remove a wedge of cake at each side so it looks as if the book is opened.

Frost top of cake with 2 c. of untinted Lemon Butter Cream.

Tint remaining frosting gold and spread on all sides of cake. Using tip 2 with remaining gold frosting, pipe parallel lines over gold base coat to represent pages.

Using yellow glossy decorating gel, write appropriate message on left side of book.

Roll out yellow gumdrops on well-sugared surface into a long strip. Cut in half lengthwise. Roll 1 strip into a tight coil for center of rose. Place other strip around coil to form petals.

Cut green gumdrops into leaves and stems. Place leaves and stems where needed to accent roses on cake. Makes 16 servings.

SWEET VIOLET CAKE

No special pan needed. Flower is cut from 13×9×2" cake

1 (13×9×2") oblong cake	**Food color**
Decorating Frosting (see	**2 green licorice sticks**
Index)	

Make a paper pattern for flower as follows: Draw a flower petal 3½" long and 2" wide, tapering to points at each end.

Use this petal pattern to make a flower with 8 petals. Cut 2 leaves from remaining cake (7" long and 1½" wide). Place flower and leaves on foil-covered bread board or cardboard.

Frost entire surface of cut pieces with a thin layer of Decorating Frosting.

Tint 2 c. Decorating Frosting pale lavender. Frost sides and top of flower, leaving a 1½" center unfrosted. Using tip 21 and remaining lavender frosting, accent edges of petals with a border.

Tint ½ c. Decorating Frosting bright yellow. Using tip 2, pipe small points close together for center of flower.

Tint remaining Decorating Frosting pale green. Spread over sides and tops of leaves. Insert green licorice sticks into flower for stem. Makes 16 servings.

7-MINUTE FROSTING

This glossy icing is a good basic recipe to keep on hand

2 egg whites
1½ c. sugar
⅓ c. water

¼ tsp. cream of tartar
1 tsp. vanilla

Combine egg whites, sugar, water and cream of tartar in top of double boiler. Beat with electric mixer at high speed 1 minute.

Place over simmering water. Cook 7 minutes, beating constantly with electric mixer at high speed until soft glossy peaks form. Remove from hot water. Stir in vanilla. Makes 2 cups.

LEMON BUTTER CREAM

Tangy icing is ideal for sponge cakes or angels, too

¾ c. shortening
¼ c. soft butter or regular
  margarine
1 (1 lb.) pkg. confectioners
  sugar

5 tsp. milk
¾ tsp. salt
2 tsp. lemon extract

Cream together shortening and butter until smooth. Gradually add confectioners sugar alternately with milk, beating well after each addition. Stir in salt and lemon extract; mix until smooth. Makes 3 cups.

CREAMY BUTTER FROSTING

A beginning cake decorator said this was easy to work with

⅓ c. soft butter or regular
  margarine
1 (1 lb.) pkg. confectioners
  sugar

5 tblsp. evaporated milk
⅛ tsp. salt
1 tsp. almond extract

Cream butter until soft and smooth. Gradually add confectioners sugar alternately with the evaporated milk, beating well after each addition. Add salt and almond extract, beating until smooth and creamy. Makes 2 cups.

CREAMY CHOCOLATE ICING

This flavorful frosting can be used for any chocolate cake

½ c. soft butter or regular margarine	2 tblsp. evaporated milk
1 (1 lb.) pkg. confectioners sugar	¼ tsp. salt
2 (1 oz.) squares unsweetened chocolate, melted	1 tsp. vanilla

Cream butter until soft and smooth. Gradually add confectioners sugar, beating well after each addition. Stir in melted chocolate, evaporated milk, salt and vanilla. Mix until smooth and creamy. Makes 2½ cups.

DECORATING FROSTING

Glossy frosting that the beginner will find easy to use

2 (1 lb.) pkgs. confectioners sugar	6 egg whites
1 tsp. cream of tartar	1 tsp. almond extract or vanilla

Pour confectioners sugar and cream of tartar into bowl. Add egg whites and almond extract. Beat with electric mixer at low speed until ingredients are well mixed. Then beat at high speed, scraping bowl occasionally, until mixture is stiff and holds its shape. Use frosting as needed. Keep unused frosting covered with wet paper towels so it will not dry out. Makes 5 cups.

Frosting can be stored in well-covered containers in the refrigerator for several weeks. *To use:* Remove from refrigerator and bring to room temperature.

Chapter 3

HOMEMADE COOKIES ...
THE FAIRS' FINEST

Always on the lookout for a new cookie recipe? Then go to the fair. There's a vast assortment of every kind of cookie imaginable, every size, shape and type . . . all arranged neatly on white paper plates. There will be puffy sugar cookies, crisp meringues, inch-high fudgy brownies, wafer-thin gingersnaps, chewy date and nut bars, golden lemon bars, crunchy coconut clusters, sturdy oatmeal raisin—to name just a few.

We have sorted the very best from cookies that have been awarded Blue and Purple Ribbons at the fairs. Many have an heirloom history. The Chocolate Drops, for example have been passed down through three generations and have captured seven Blues. The Glazed Butterscotch Brownies and the Milk Chocolate Brownies are both originals from fine farm cooks—both look special enough to serve at a fancy tea.

The Governor's Cookie Jar always draws keen competition and a big crowd at the Kansas fair. This is an entry class for Best Cookie Jar. We interviewed the happy winner. She thought her cookie recipes were prize-winning material but she was a bit concerned about the design of her gallon jar (the judging is on both the original jar design and the excellence of the cookies). "Frankly, I didn't look at any of the other entries for the decorated jars so I really didn't know what to expect." She admitted she certainly *didn't* expect to be in Hutchinson on a Tuesday afternoon presenting her cookie jar to the governor—but she was:

"I filled my jar with fifteen kinds of cookies—recipes I always make at Christmas time. Three of them were exchanges from friends and the rest I have picked up and revised to suit my family's tastes."

Many of the women who entered their cookies came away with a White Ribbon, third prize or with no ribbon at all. Disappointed but not discouraged, they were determined to try again next year, which is the true spirit of fair competition. However, they wondered why their cookies weren't up to par this year. We have tried to answer some questions on how to perfect cookies to Blue Ribbon standards.

Meanwhile we hope you will make and munch all of the cookies in this chapter as we have carefully tested and perfected them to our FARM JOURNAL Test Kitchen standards.

How to Judge a Perfect Bar Cookie

A bar cookie is cake-like in texture and is made from a stiff batter which has been evenly spread in a shallow pan. After baking, they are cut into bars or squares. A perfect bar cookie has uniform size, well-cut shape, rich moist interior and a thin delicate crust.

COMMON PROBLEMS WITH BAR COOKIES . . . AND PROBABLE CAUSES

Dry and crumbly—overbaking.
Hard crusty top—overmixing.
Crumbly texture—cut while bars are too warm.

How to Judge a Perfect Refrigerator Cookie

A refrigerator cookie is made from a fairly rich dough which has been shaped into a roll and chilled thoroughly. A perfect refrigerator cookie should be rich and flavorful with a uniform well-cut shape, lightly browned surface and a crisp crunchy texture.

COMMON PROBLEMS WITH REFRIGERATOR COOKIES . . . AND PROBABLE CAUSES

Irregular shape—improper molding of dough roll, insufficient chilling of dough, or dull knife used when slicing.
Too brown—overbaking.
Soft—cut too thick.

How to Judge a Perfect Rolled Cookie

Rolled cookies are made from a slightly stiff dough and rolled out lightly on a floured board to desired thickness and shape. An excellent rolled cookie should retain the shape of the cutter, have slightly browned edges and be crisp and tender.

COMMON PROBLEMS WITH ROLLED COOKIES . . . AND PROBABLE CAUSES

Toughness—excessive rolling.
Visible flour on surface—too much flour used when rolling out dough.
Dryness—too much flour used when rolling out dough, or re-rolling of dough.

How to Judge a Perfect Drop Cookie

Dropped cookies are made from a soft dough and are dropped from a spoon onto a baking sheet. They may or may not be flattened. An excellent drop cookie has a fairly uniform mound shape, a delicate brown exterior, interesting texture and good flavor.

COMMON PROBLEMS WITH DROPPED COOKIES . . . AND PROBABLE CAUSES

Irregular size and shape—dough was dropped unevenly.
Dark crusty edges—overbaking.

Dryness and hardness—overbaking.

Doughiness—underbaking.

Excessive spreading—dough too warm, baking sheet too hot, incorrect oven temperature, or failure to peak the top when dough was dropped onto baking sheet.

Tips to Help You Bake a Perfect Cookie

Use shiny baking sheets. Darkened or dull baking sheets absorb heat and may result in the bottom of the cookie becoming too brown.

Bake one sheet at a time for best results.

Cool sheets in between bakings to prevent dough from spreading.

To save time if you are baking several batches of cookies, cut a piece of heavy-duty aluminum foil to fit the baking sheet. You will be able to slide the foil onto the warm baking sheet and pop into the oven.

Cool cookies thoroughly on a wire rack. Do not overlap as this will cause cookies to stick together and lose their shape.

Use a pastry cloth when rolling out cookie dough. This will prevent dough from sticking. Don't use too much flour—a pastry cloth helps to prevent picking up extra flour, which produces a dry and hard cookie.

Bake cookies that are high in shortening on an ungreased baking sheet and those low in shortening on a greased sheet.

When baking refrigerator cookies if both dough and baking sheet are cold, the cookies will be easier to mold and will retain their shape.

Store soft cookies in a tightly covered container. A slice of apple, orange or bread helps keep cookies moist. Store crisp cookies in a loosely covered container.

BROWNIES AND MORE BROWNIES

Thick fudgy brownies, soft cake-like brownies, orange-flavored brownies, creamy-layered brownies, delicately flavored light chocolate brownies, rich robust chocolate brownies—these are just a few of the Blue Ribbon winners that we present in this richly delicious section.

First there's a buttery Butterscotch Brownie which the Indiana Blue Ribbon winner says are different and delicious. Extra-good spread with a thin layer of melted chocolate, too.

"I'm always expected to bring two batches of my Fudge Cinnamon Brownies to our potluck suppers," says the Kansas winner of two Blue Ribbons. "My children think they taste like homemade fudge."

In Nebraska, a winner with her Honey Brownies told us that her family prefers the gentle chocolate flavor of these brownies.

"My boys practically inhale my Chocolate Brownie Bars—I always have to hide them until it's time for dessert," says a Minnesota winner. "I've won two Blue Ribbons but my family gave them a Blue Ribbon rating long before that."

BUTTERSCOTCH BROWNIES

The special frosting makes these brownies different

¼ c. melted butter or regular margarine	½ tsp. salt
	½ c. chopped walnuts
1 c. brown sugar, firmly packed	2 (1 oz.) squares semi-sweet chocolate
1 egg	2 tblsp. butter or regular margarine
½ tsp. vanilla	
1 c. sifted flour	Brown Butter Frosting (recipe follows)
1 tsp. baking powder	

Combine ¼ c. melted butter and brown sugar; mix until thoroughly blended. Stir in egg and vanilla.

Sift together flour, baking powder and salt. Stir into brown sugar mixture. Add walnuts. Spread mixture in greased 8″ square baking pan.

Bake in 350° oven 30 minutes or until done. Cool in pan on rack.

Melt chocolate and 2 tblsp. butter together over low heat, stirring constantly. Cool slightly.

Spread with Brown Butter Frosting. Pour chocolate mixture

over top, slightly tilting pan back and forth to distribute chocolate over surface. When toppings are set, cut in 2½ ×1½″ bars. Makes 15 bars.

Brown Butter Frosting: Melt ¼ c. butter or regular margarine over low heat to a light golden brown; remove from heat. Blend in 2 c. sifted confectioners sugar. Stir in 2 tblsp. light cream and 1 tsp. vanilla; blend until smooth and of spreading consistency.

FUDGE CINNAMON BROWNIES

A large batch of brownies . . . perfect for a crowd

2 c. sifted flour	2 eggs
2 c. sugar	1 tsp. vanilla
1 c. butter or regular	1 tsp. baking soda
margarine	1 tsp. ground cinnamon
7 tblsp. cocoa	Chocolate Fudge Frosting
1 c. water	(recipe follows)
½ c. buttermilk	1 c. chopped pecans

Sift together flour and sugar into bowl.

Mix together butter, cocoa and water in a heavy saucepan. Bring to a boil over medium heat. Slowly pour mixture over flour and sugar, blending with electric mixer. Add buttermilk, eggs, vanilla, baking soda and cinnamon; mix well. Spread in greased 15½ ×10½ ×1″ jelly roll pan.

Bake in 400° oven 20 minutes or until done. Cool in pan on rack. Frost with Chocolate Fudge Frosting. Sprinkle with pecans. Cut in 2″ squares. Makes 35 squares.

Chocolate Fudge Frosting: Melt ½ c. butter or regular margarine in 2-qt. heavy saucepan. Add 5 tblsp. cocoa and 6 tblsp. milk; stir well. Bring mixture to a boil. Remove from heat. Add 1 (1 lb.) pkg. confectioners sugar and 1 tsp. vanilla; beat until smooth.

HONEY BROWNIES

Mild chocolate flavor of these brownies makes them good

⅓ c. butter or regular margarine	1 tsp. vanilla
2 (1 oz.) squares unsweetened chocolate	¾ c. sifted flour
	½ tsp. baking powder
2 eggs	¼ tsp. salt
½ c. honey	½ c. chopped walnuts
½ c. sugar	Confectioners sugar

Melt together butter and chocolate over hot water; cool.

Beat eggs slightly in bowl. Add honey, sugar and vanilla; beat well. Add chocolate mixture; blend well.

Sift together flour, baking powder and salt. Gradually add dry ingredients to creamed mixture; mix well. Stir in walnuts. Spread batter in greased and floured 9″ square baking pan.

Bake in 350° oven 25 minutes. Cool in pan on rack. Cut in 3×1″ bars. Roll in confectioners sugar. Makes 2 dozen.

CHOCOLATE BROWNIE BARS

The creamy chocolate frosting makes these so extra-good

½ c. butter or regular margarine	½ tsp. baking powder
	1 (1 lb.) can chocolate-flavored syrup
1 c. sugar	
4 eggs	Chocolate Frosting (recipe follows)
1 c. sifted flour	

Cream together butter and sugar until light and fluffy. Blend in eggs, one at a time, beating well after each addition.

Sift together flour and baking powder. Gradually add dry ingredients to creamed mixture; mix well. Blend in chocolate syrup. Pour into greased and floured 9″ square baking pan.

Bake in 350° oven 35 minutes or until done. Cool in pan on rack. Spread with Chocolate Frosting. Cut in 3×1″ bars. Makes about 2 dozen.

Chocolate Frosting: Combine 2 c. sifted confectioners sugar, 1 tblsp. butter, ½ tsp. vanilla and 1 (1 oz.) square unsweetened chocolate, melted. Add enough milk (about 2 tblsp.) to make a frosting of spreading consistency.

MILK CHOCOLATE BROWNIES

No need to frost these brownies—the topping is baked on

½ c. butter or regular
　margarine
2 c. sugar
4 eggs
2 tsp. vanilla
1½ c. sifted flour
½ c. cocoa

½ tsp. salt
1 c. flaked coconut
½ c. semi-sweet chocolate
　pieces
2 tblsp. sugar
½ c. chopped walnuts

Melt butter in saucepan over low heat. Add 2 c. sugar; beat well. Mix in eggs and vanilla; blend well.

Sift together flour, cocoa and salt. Add to sugar mixture and mix thoroughly. Stir in coconut. Spread in greased 13×9×2" baking pan.

Combine chocolate pieces, 2 tblsp. sugar and walnuts; sprinkle evenly over batter.

Bake in 350° oven 25 minutes or until done. Cool in pan on rack. Cut in 2½×1" bars. Makes 2 dozen.

BEST-EVER BROWNIES

Avid chocolate fans will like these chewy, moist brownies

½ c. butter or regular
　margarine
1 c. sugar
2 eggs
1 tsp. vanilla
2 (1 oz.) squares
　unsweetened chocolate,
　melted

¾ c. sifted flour
½ tsp. baking powder
¼ tsp. salt
1 c. chopped walnuts
¼ c. confectioners sugar

Cream together butter and sugar until light and fluffy. Add eggs, one at a time, beating well after each addition. Blend in vanilla and chocolate.

Sift together flour, baking powder and salt. Add to creamed mixture, blending well. Stir in walnuts. Spread in greased 9" square baking pan. Dust confectioners sugar evenly over top.

Bake in 350° oven 35 minutes or until done. Cool in pan on rack. Cut in 1½" squares. Makes 25 squares.

CHOCOLATE FUDGE SQUARES

Tuck these moist brownies into packed lunches for a treat

2 (1 oz.) squares unsweetened chocolate	1 tsp. vanilla
	½ c. sifted flour
½ c. shortening	¼ tsp. salt
1 c. sugar	½ c. coarsely chopped walnuts
2 eggs, beaten	

Melt chocolate and shortening over low heat; stir until smooth. Cool.

Stir in sugar, mixing thoroughly. Add eggs; beat well. Add vanilla.

Sift together flour and salt; add to chocolate mixture, blending well. Spread in greased 9" square baking pan. Sprinkle with walnuts.

Bake in 400° oven 18 minutes or until done. Cool in pan on rack. Cut in 1½" squares. Makes 3 dozen.

FUDGE WALNUT BROWNIES

These delicious brownies have been fair winners for six years

½ c. butter or regular margarine	1 tsp. vanilla
	¾ c. sifted flour
2 (1 oz.) squares unsweetened chocolate	½ tsp. baking powder
	¼ tsp. salt
2 eggs	¾ c. chopped walnuts
1 c. sugar	

Melt butter and chocolate over low heat. Cool.

Beat eggs slightly. Blend in sugar, vanilla and chocolate mixture.

Sift together flour, baking powder and salt. Stir into chocolate mixture. Add walnuts. Spread in greased 11×7×1½" baking dish.

Bake in 350° oven 30 minutes or until done. Cool in pan on rack. Cut in 2×1" bars. Makes 2½ dozen.

CHOCOLATE CHIP BLONDE BROWNIES

Serve these light brownies with mugs of frothy hot chocolate

⅓ c. melted butter or regular margarine	¾ c. sifted flour
	½ tsp. baking powder
¾ c. brown sugar, firmly packed	¼ tsp. baking soda
	½ tsp. salt
1 egg	½ c. semi-sweet chocolate pieces
1 tsp. vanilla	

Combine butter, brown sugar, egg and vanilla; mix well.

Sift together flour, baking powder, baking soda and salt. Stir into brown sugar mixture; blend well. Stir in chocolate pieces. Spread in greased 8" square baking pan.

Bake in 350° oven 20 minutes or until done. Cool in pan on rack. Cut in 2½×1" bars. Makes 2 dozen.

DELECTABLE CHOCOLATE BROWNIES

These rich, moist brownies keep well for several days

¾ c. butter or regular margarine	¾ c. sifted flour
	½ c. cocoa
1½ c. sugar	¼ tsp. salt
2 eggs	¾ c. chopped walnuts
½ tsp. vanilla	

Cream together butter and sugar until light and fluffy. Add eggs and vanilla; beat well.

Sift together flour, cocoa and salt. Add to creamed mixture, blending well. Stir in walnuts. Spread in greased 9″ square baking pan.

Bake in 350° oven 35 minutes or until done. Cool in pan on rack. Cut 2¾ ×1¾″ bars. Makes 15.

FREEZE-AHEAD FAVORITES

"I aways keep at least three rolls of my Chocolate Fair Cookies in my freezer," a Nebraska winner wrote us. "This is an heirloom hand-me-down through three generations." Wafer-thin, extra crisp, this cookie has a deep-dark appearance and flavor.

Three sugar cookies, all delicately golden edged with crisp brown rims, are sure favorites all year round. And they all have won Blue Ribbons—Crisp Sugar Cookies from Arkansas with just a hint of nutmeg, Basic Sugar Cookies from Ohio and Rolled Sugar Cookies from North Dakota. You will want to freeze one batch of each as they all taste different.

Serve Chinese Almond Cookies as a finale after a Chinese dinner. They have won several Blues at a Washington fair.

CHOCOLATE FAIR COOKIES

A three-generation recipe that is a real family favorite

½ c. shortening	1½ tsp. baking powder
1 c. sugar	½ tsp. baking soda
1 egg	½ tsp. ground cinnamon
3 (1 oz.) squares	½ tsp. salt
unsweetened chocolate,	2 tblsp. milk
melted	Sugar
2 c. sifted cake flour	

Cream together shortening and 1 c. sugar until light and fluffy. Add egg and melted chocolate; beat well.

Sift together cake flour, baking powder, baking soda, cinnamon and salt. Add dry ingredients to creamed mixture, a little at a time, mixing well after each addition. Add milk. Chill dough in refrigerator 8 hours or overnight.

Roll dough about ⅛" thick on lightly floured surface. Cut with floured 2½" cookie cutter. Place about 2" apart on ungreased baking sheets. Sprinkle each with sugar.

Bake in 350° oven 9 minutes or until done. Remove from baking sheets; cool on racks. Makes about 4 dozen.

CRISP SUGAR COOKIES

Mild nutmeg flavor makes these crunchy cookies good

2 c. sugar	2 tsp. baking powder
1 c. butter or regular	1 tsp. baking soda
margarine	1 tsp. salt
4 eggs	1 tsp. ground nutmeg
4½ c. sifted flour	2 tblsp. milk

Cream together sugar and shortening until light and fluffy. Add eggs, one at a time, beating well after each addition.

Sift together flour, baking powder, baking soda, salt and nutmeg. Add dry ingredients alternately with milk to creamed mixture; mix well. Chill dough in refrigerator 2 to 3 hours.

Roll dough ⅛ to ¼" thick on floured surface. Cut with floured 2" cookie cutter. Place about 2" apart on greased baking sheets.

Bake in 425° oven 8 to 10 minutes or until golden brown. Cool about 1 minute on baking sheets. Remove from baking sheets; cool on racks. Makes 6 dozen.

BASIC SUGAR COOKIES

Serve with sugared, cut-up fresh fruit for a simple dessert

½ c. butter or regular	2½ c. sifted flour
margarine	3 tsp. baking powder
1 c. sugar	½ tsp. salt
2 eggs	Sugar
1 tsp. vanilla	

Cream together butter and 1 c. sugar until light and fluffy. Add eggs, one at a time, beating well after each addition. Add vanilla.

Sift together flour, baking powder and salt. Gradually add dry ingredients to creamed mixture, mixing well. Chill dough in refrigerator 1 hour.

Roll dough ¼ to ⅜″ thick on lightly floured surface. Cut with floured 2″ cookie cutter. Place about 2″ apart on ungreased baking sheets. Sprinkle tops with sugar.

Bake in 400° oven 8 to 10 minutes or until golden brown. Remove from baking sheets; cool on racks. Makes 4½ dozen.

ROLLED SUGAR COOKIES

These golden cookies won a Purple Ribbon in North Dakota

2 eggs	2 tsp. cream of tartar
1 c. sugar	1 tsp. baking soda
1 tsp. vanilla	1 c. butter or regular
3 c. sifted flour	margarine

Beat eggs thoroughly. Add sugar and vanilla; beat well.

Sift together flour, cream of tartar and baking soda. Cut in butter until mixture is crumbly. Add egg mixture, stirring until dough is moist enough to hold together. Chill in refrigerator 20 minutes.

Roll dough ¼″ thick on lightly floured surface. Cut with floured 2″ cookie cutter. Place about 2″ apart on greased baking sheets.

Bake in 400° oven 8 to 10 minutes or until golden brown. Remove from baking sheets; cool on racks. Makes about 5½ dozen.

CHINESE ALMOND COOKIES

This Oregon woman won three ribbons on cookies in one year

1 c. butter or regular	3 c. sifted flour
margarine	1 tsp. baking powder
1½ c. sugar	¼ tsp. salt
1 egg	½ c. chopped, toasted
1 tsp. almond extract	almonds
½ tsp. vanilla	

Cream together butter and sugar until light and fluffy. Add egg, almond extract and vanilla; blend well.

Sift together flour, baking powder and salt. Gradually add dry ingredients to creamed mixture; mix well.

Roll dough about ¼" thick on lightly floured surface. Cut with floured 2" round cookie cutter. Place rounds about 2" apart on greased baking sheets. Sprinkle with almonds. Press almonds down lightly into each round.

Bake in 325° oven 15 minutes or until golden brown. Remove from baking sheets; cool on racks. Makes 4 dozen.

ALMOND COOKIES

This winner added her personal touch by making them square

**1 c. butter or regular
    margarine**
½ c. sugar
2 tblsp. water
½ tsp. vanilla
1 tsp. almond extract

2 c. sifted flour
½ tsp. baking powder
**½ c. chopped, toasted
    almonds**
Sugar

Cream together butter, ½ c. sugar, water, vanilla and almond extract.

Sift together flour and baking powder; add to creamed mixture, mixing thoroughly. Add almonds; mix well. Chill 1 hour. Use an empty 12" long plastic wrap, waxed paper or aluminum foil carton. Grease a 10" long sheet of waxed paper and place in carton. Press dough into carton. Wrap waxed paper securely around dough. Chill 8 hours or overnight.

Cut rolls in ¼" slices. Place about 2" apart on ungreased baking sheets.

Bake in 350° oven 12 to 15 minutes or until golden brown. Remove from baking sheets and roll in sugar. Remove from pans; cool on racks. Makes about 4 dozen.

GERMAN SUGAR COOKIES

No need to chill the dough . . . it's so easy to work with

1 c. butter or regular margarine	3 c. sifted flour
1 c. sugar	½ tsp. baking powder
2 eggs	½ tsp. baking soda
1 tsp. vanilla	¼ tsp. salt

Cream together butter and sugar until light and fluffy. Add eggs, one at a time, beating well after each addition. Blend in vanilla.

Sift together flour, baking powder, baking soda and salt. Add dry ingredients to creamed mixture, blending well.

Roll dough about ¼" thick on lightly floured surface. Cut with floured 2" cookie cutters. Place about 2" apart on greased baking sheets.

Bake in 350° oven 10 to 12 minutes or until golden brown. Remove from baking sheets; cool on racks. Makes 6 dozen.

GRAPE SWIRL COOKIES

At Christmastime, fill cookies with mincemeat instead

¾ c. grape jam	⅔ c. sugar
1 c. chopped walnuts	2 eggs
1½ c. chopped seedless raisins	1 tsp. vanilla
1 c. butter or regular margarine	3½ c. sifted flour
1 c. brown sugar, firmly packed	1 tsp. baking powder
	1 tsp. salt
	¼ tsp. baking soda

Combine jam, walnuts and raisins for filling; set aside.

Cream together butter and sugars until light and fluffy. Add eggs, one at a time, beating well after each addition. Add vanilla.

Sift together flour, baking powder, salt and baking soda; add to creamed mixture, mixing thoroughly. Divide dough in half.

Roll each half into 13×9″ rectangle on lightly floured surface. Spread half of filling over each rectangle. Roll up like jelly roll starting from long side. Wrap tightly in plastic wrap or waxed paper. Refrigerate 8 hours or overnight.

With a knife that has been dipped in water, cut dough quickly in ¼″ slices. Place 2″ apart on well-greased baking sheets.

Bake in 400° oven 12 minutes or until golden brown. Remove from baking sheets immediately; cool on racks. Makes about 8½ dozen.

Note: Be sure to work quickly when cutting dough in slices. Return remaining roll to refrigerator between bakings.

REFRIGERATED DATE COOKIES

Chewy date cookies that were a ribbon winner in Tennessee

1 c. cut-up dates	3 eggs
1 c. sugar	4 c. sifted flour
1 c. water	½ tsp. baking soda
1 c. chopped walnuts	½ tsp. salt
1 c. shortening	
2 c. brown sugar, firmly packed	

Combine dates, sugar and water in small saucepan. Cook over medium heat, stirring constantly, until mixture thickens. Remove from heat; cool. Stir in walnuts; set aside.

Cream together shortening and brown sugar until light and fluffy. Add eggs, one at a time, beating well after each addition.

Sift together flour, baking soda and salt. Gradually add dry ingredients to creamed mixture, mixing well. Chill dough in refrigerator 1 hour. Divide dough in half. Roll each half into 13×9″ rectangle on lightly floured surface. Spread with half of filling. Roll up like a jelly roll starting from long side. Refrigerate 8 hours or overnight.

Cut dough in ¼″ slices. Place about 2″ apart on greased baking sheets.

Bake in 400° oven 10 minutes or until golden brown. Remove from baking sheets; cool on racks. Makes 7 dozen.

DATE PINWHEELS

Unbaked cookie rolls can be refrigerated several days

1 c. cut-up dates
1 c. water
½ c. sugar
1 c. chopped walnuts
1 c. shortening
1 c. brown sugar, firmly
   packed

1 c. sugar
3 eggs
1 tsp. vanilla
3 c. sifted flour
1 tsp. baking powder
1 tsp. baking soda
¼ tsp. salt

Combine dates, water and ½ c. sugar in small saucepan. Cook over medium heat, stirring constantly, until mixture thickens. Remove from heat; stir in walnuts. Set filling aside.

Cream together shortening, brown sugar and 1 c. sugar until light and fluffy. Add eggs, one at a time, beating well after each addition. Add vanilla.

Sift together flour, baking powder, baking soda and salt. Gradually add dry ingredients to creamed mixture; mix well. Chill dough in refrigerator 2 hours.

Divide dough in fourths. Roll each part into 10×6" rectangle. Spread each with ¼ of date filling. Roll up like a jelly roll from long side. Chill overnight.

Cut dough in ⅛" slices. Place about 2" apart on greased baking sheets.

Bake in 350° oven 10 to 12 minutes or until done. Remove from baking sheets; cool on racks. Makes 11 dozen.

OATMEAL REFRIGERATOR COOKIES

A winner the last two years at a county fair in New York

1 c. shortening
1 c. sugar
1 c. brown sugar, firmly
   packed
2 eggs, well beaten

2 tsp. vanilla
1½ c. sifted flour
1 tsp. baking soda
½ tsp. salt
3 c. quick-cooking oats

Cream together shortening and sugars until light and fluffy. Add eggs, one at a time, beating well after each addition. Blend in vanilla.

Sift together flour, baking soda and salt. Gradually add dry ingredients to creamed mixture; mix well. Stir in oats.

Divide dough in thirds. Shape into 10×1¼" rolls. Wrap tightly in plastic wrap or waxed paper. Chill several hours or overnight.

Cut rolls in thin slices. Place about 1½" apart on ungreased baking sheets.

Bake in 400° oven 6 to 8 minutes or until done. Remove from baking sheets. Cool on racks. Makes about 8 dozen.

CRUNCHY BUTTERSCOTCH COOKIES

Prize-winning cookies at a recent Arkansas county fair

¾ c. butter or regular margarine	2 c. sifted flour
1 c. brown sugar, firmly packed	½ tsp. cream of tartar
	½ tsp. baking soda
1 egg	½ tsp. salt
1 tsp. vanilla	1 c. chopped walnuts

Cream together butter and brown sugar until light and fluffy. Add egg and vanilla; beat well.

Sift together flour, cream of tartar, baking soda and salt. Gradually add dry ingredients to creamed mixture; mix well. Stir in walnuts. Shape dough into a roll 1½" in diameter. Wrap tightly in plastic wrap or waxed paper. Chill several hours or overnight.

Cut dough in ¼" slices. Place about 1½" apart on greased baking sheets.

Bake in 400° oven 10 minutes or until golden brown. Remove from baking sheets. Cool on racks. Makes 4½ dozen.

LUNCH BOX SPECIALS

Children like soft chewy cookies that are easy to handle and this section provides the recipes. They will love the Oatmeal Date Cookies—a big fat cookie from Wisconsin, soft puffy Raisin Cookies from Washington, Buttermilk Chocolate Chip from Idaho. All won a Blue Ribbon at state fairs.

Then there's a good choice of chocolate cookies men especially like. "No matter where we take these Chocolate Cookies, they disappear," states a Blue Ribbon winner from Wisconsin.

OATMEAL DATE COOKIES

"Best oatmeals I've ever tasted," one tester commented

1 c. shortening	1 tsp. baking powder
1 c. brown sugar, firmly packed	¾ tsp. baking soda
1 c. sugar	½ tsp. salt
3 eggs	2 c. quick-cooking oats
1 tsp. vanilla	½ c. chopped walnuts
2 c. sifted flour	1 c. cut-up dates
	1 c. flaked coconut

Cream together shortening and sugars until light and fluffy. Add eggs, one at a time, beating well after each addition. Blend in vanilla.

Sift together flour, baking powder, baking soda and salt. Gradually add dry ingredients to creamed mixture; mix well. Stir in oats, walnuts, dates and coconut. Drop by teaspoonfuls about 2" apart on greased baking sheets. Flatten with bottom of drinking glass dipped in sugar.

Bake in 375° oven 8 minutes or until lightly browned. Remove from baking sheets; cool on racks. Makes 5 dozen.

RAISIN COOKIES

Good basic cookies . . . add cinnamon for a change of pace

1 c. shortening	¼ tsp. salt
1½ c. sugar	¼ tsp. ground nutmeg
3 eggs	½ c. hot water
1 tsp. vanilla	1 c. raisins or currants
3 c. sifted flour	1 tblsp. flour
1 tsp. baking soda	

Cream together shortening and sugar until light and fluffy. Add eggs, one at a time, beating well after each addition. Beat in vanilla.

Sift together 3 c. flour, baking soda, salt and nutmeg. Add dry ingredients alternately with hot water to creamed mixture, mixing well after each addition.

Combine raisins and 1 tblsp. flour. Stir into dough. Drop dough by teaspoonfuls about 2″ apart on greased baking sheets.

Bake in 400° oven 10 minutes or until golden brown. Remove from baking sheets. Cool on racks. Makes about 5 dozen.

BUTTERMILK CHOCOLATE CHIP COOKIES

Blue Ribbon winner at the county and state levels in Idaho

1 c. shortening	3 c. sifted flour
1 c. sugar	1 tsp. baking soda
1 c. brown sugar, firmly packed	½ c. buttermilk
2 eggs	1 (6 oz.) pkg. semi-sweet chocolate pieces
1½ tsp. vanilla	1 c. chopped walnuts

Cream together shortening and sugars until light and fluffy. Beat in eggs one at a time. Blend in vanilla.

Sift together flour and baking soda. Add dry ingredients alternately with buttermilk to creamed mixture; mix well. Stir in chocolate pieces and walnuts. Drop by teaspoonfuls about 2″ apart on greased baking sheets.

Bake in 350° oven 12 to 15 minutes or until done. Remove from baking sheets; cool on racks. Makes 7 dozen.

CHOCOLATE COOKIES

Cookies won a Blue Ribbon for a 4-H food project leader

½ c. shortening	¾ tsp. salt
1 c. sugar	3 (1 oz.) squares
2 eggs	unsweetened chocolate,
1 tsp. vanilla	melted
¾ c. sifted flour	

Cream together shortening and sugar until light and fluffy. Add eggs, one at a time, beating well after each addition. Beat in vanilla.

Sift together flour and salt. Gradually add dry ingredients to creamed mixture; mix well. Blend in chocolate. Drop by teaspoonfuls about 2" apart on greased baking sheets.

Bake in 325° oven 15 minutes or until done. Remove from baking sheets; cool on racks. If you wish, frost with butter cream frosting and decorate each with a maraschino cherry half. Makes about 2½ dozen.

CHOCOLATE DROP COOKIES

Cookies can be decorated with chopped nuts before baking

1 (6 oz.) pkg. semi-sweet chocolate pieces	1 c. sifted flour
½ c. butter or regular margarine	½ tsp. baking soda
½ c. sugar	½ tsp. salt
1 egg	½ c. chopped walnuts
	1 (6 oz.) pkg. semi-sweet chocolate pieces

Melt 1 (6 oz.) pkg. semi-sweet chocolate pieces over low heat. Set aside to cool.

Cream together butter and sugar until light and fluffy. Add egg; beat well. Gradually add melted chocolate, beating well.

Sift together flour, baking soda and salt. Gradually add dry ingredients to creamed mixture; mix well. Stir in walnuts and remaining package of chocolate pieces. Drop by teaspoonfuls about 2″ apart on greased baking sheets.

Bake in 350° oven 12 to 15 minutes or until done. Remove from baking sheets; cool on racks. Makes 4 dozen.

COCONUT DATE COOKIES

Called "men's cookies" by the homemaker that developed them

1 c. butter or shortening	1 tsp. baking powder
1 c. sugar	1 tsp. baking soda
1 c. brown sugar, firmly packed	1 tsp. salt
	2 c. quick-cooking oats
2 eggs	1 c. finely chopped dates
1 tsp. vanilla	1 c. broken walnuts
2 c. sifted flour	1 c. flaked coconut

Cream together butter and sugars until light and fluffy. Add eggs, one at a time, beating well after each addition. Blend in vanilla.

Sift together flour, baking powder, baking soda and salt. Gradually add dry ingredients to creamed mixture; mix well. Stir in oats, dates, walnuts and coconut. Chill dough in refrigerator 1 hour. Drop by teaspoonfuls about 2″ apart on greased baking sheets.

Bake in 350° oven 12 to 15 minutes or until done. Remove from baking sheets; cool on racks. Makes about 6 dozen.

CHEWY OATMEAL DROPS

For extra flavor, use bacon fat for half of shortening

1 c. shortening	2 c. sifted flour
2 c. brown sugar, firmly packed	1 tsp. salt
	1 tsp. baking soda
2 eggs	¼ c. boiling water
1 tsp. vanilla	2 c. quick-cooking oats

Cream together shortening and brown sugar until light and fluffy. Add eggs, one at a time, beating well after each addition. Blend in vanilla.

Sift together flour and salt.

Combine baking soda and boiling water. Add dry ingredients alternately with soda mixture to creamed mixture; mix well. Stir in oats. Drop by teaspoonfuls about 2" apart on greased baking sheets.

Bake in 350° oven 12 minutes or until done. Cool slightly on baking sheets. Remove from baking sheets; cool on racks. Makes about 5 dozen.

NUT RAISIN COOKIES

Crunchy cookies that will especially appeal to children

½ c. shortening	1½ c. sifted flour
½ c. brown sugar, firmly packed	½ tsp. baking soda
	½ tsp. salt
¼ c. sugar	3 tblsp. water
1 egg	½ c. chopped walnuts
½ tsp. vanilla	½ c. raisins

Cream together shortening and sugars until light and fluffy. Add egg and vanilla; beat well.

Sift together flour, baking soda and salt. Add dry ingredients alternately with water to creamed mixture, beating well after each addition. Stir in walnuts and raisins. Drop by teaspoonfuls about 2" apart on ungreased baking sheets. Sprinkle tops with sugar.

Bake in 375° oven 10 minutes or until done. Remove from baking sheets; cool on racks. Makes about 3 dozen.

FROSTED CHOCOLATE DROPS

Children will like these cookies with milk after school

1 c. shortening	¼ c. cocoa
2 c. brown sugar, firmly packed	1 tsp. baking soda
	1 tsp. salt
2 eggs	1 c. milk
2 tsp. vanilla	Mocha Frosting (recipe follows)
3⅓ c. sifted flour	

Cream together shortening and brown sugar until light and fluffy. Add eggs, one at a time, beating well after each addition. Blend in vanilla.

Sift together flour, cocoa, baking soda and salt. Add dry ingredients alternately with milk to creamed mixture, beating well after each addition. Drop by teaspoonfuls about 2" apart on greased baking sheets.

Bake in 350° oven 10 minutes or until done. Remove from baking sheets; cool on racks. Frost with Mocha Frosting. Makes about 7 dozen.

Mocha Frosting: Combine ¼ c. cocoa, ½ c. soft butter or regular margarine, 1 tsp. vanilla and 3 c. sifted confectioners sugar. Gradually stir in ¼ c. hot coffee. Beat until smooth and of spreading consistency.

BROWNIE DROP COOKIES

A homemaker in Wisconsin makes these cookies once a week

1 c. butter or regular	½ c. cocoa
margarine	1 tsp. baking powder
1¾ c. sugar	1 tsp. baking soda
1 c. creamed cottage cheese	½ tsp. salt
2 eggs	½ c. chopped pecans
1 tsp. vanilla	Creamy Frosting (recipe
2½ c. sifted flour	follows)

Cream butter and sugar until light and fluffy. Add cottage cheese; beat thoroughly. Add eggs, one at a time, beating well after each addition. Blend in vanilla.

Sift together flour, cocoa, baking powder, baking soda and salt. Gradually add dry ingredients to creamed mixture; mix well. Stir in pecans. Drop by teaspoonfuls about 2" apart on greased baking sheets.

Bake in 350° oven 12 minutes or until done. Remove from baking sheets; cool on racks. Frost with Creamy Frosting. Makes 6 dozen.

Creamy Frosting: Combine 2½ c. sifted confectioners sugar,

¼ c. softened butter or regular margarine, ¼ c. light cream and 1 tsp. vanilla. Beat until smooth and of spreading consistency.

FUDGE WALNUT COOKIES

Keep in the freezer for spur-of-the-moment entertaining

1½ c. shortening	2 tsp. baking powder
3⅓ c. sugar	1 tsp. baking soda
4 eggs	1 tsp. salt
2 c. creamed cottage cheese	1 c. chopped walnuts
4 tsp. vanilla	1 (6 oz.) pkg. semi-sweet
5½ c. sifted flour	chocolate pieces
1 c. cocoa	Confectioners sugar

Cream together shortening and sugar until light and fluffy. Add eggs, one at a time, beating well after each addition. Blend in cottage cheese and vanilla.

Sift together flour, cocoa, baking powder, baking soda and salt. Gradually add dry ingredients to creamed mixture; mix well. Stir in walnuts and chocolate pieces. Drop by teaspoonfuls about 2″ apart on greased baking sheets.

Bake in 350° oven 12 to 15 minutes or until done. Remove from baking sheets. Roll in confectioners sugar while still warm. Cool on racks. Makes about 11 dozen.

ESPECIALLY FOR BAZAARS AND BAKE SALES

"Whenever we have a bake sale, I am expected to bring at least four batches of my Honey Raisin Bars and they are usually sold in less than thirty minutes," wrote a busy homemaker from Idaho. "After a back-yard barbecue, I serve them with fruit and ice cream for company dessert, and both children and grownups never fail to come back for seconds." These snowy drifts of sweetness certainly rate the Blue Ribbon they won.

From Alaska, a Blue Ribbon winner, Northern Light Bars are rich and tartly lemon with a creamy cheese filling and a crunchy top. Maple Walnut Squares, winner from Kansas, taste like crackly pecan candy.

Laced with coffee, crunchy with nuts and raisins, Coffee-flavored Cookie Squares picked up two Blue Ribbons at Minnesota fairs.

We think all these bar cookies will quickly disappear when you bring them to your next bake sale.

HONEY RAISIN BARS

Serve for dessert with frosty lemon sherbet

1½ c. shortening	2 tsp. salt
1 c. sugar	3 tsp. ground cinnamon
1 c. brown sugar, firmly	1 tsp. ground cardamom
packed	1 tsp. ground nutmeg
1 c. honey	1 tsp. ground allspice
3 eggs	1½ c. quick-cooking oats
2 tsp. vanilla	2 c. raisins
3½ c. sifted flour	1 c. chopped walnuts
2 tsp. baking soda	Confectioners sugar

Cream together shortening and sugars until light and fluffy. Beat in honey, eggs and vanilla; blend well.

Sift together flour, baking soda, salt, cinnamon, cardamom, nutmeg and allspice. Gradually add dry ingredients to creamed mixture; mix well. Stir in oats, raisins and walnuts. Spread mixture in 2 greased 15½ ×10½ ×1″ jelly roll pans.

Bake in 375° oven 18 minutes or until done. Cool in pans on racks. Cut in 2×1″ bars. (Each pan makes 80 bars.) Roll in confectioners sugar. Makes about 13 dozen.

NORTHERN LIGHT BARS

An Alaska homemaker won top prize with these buttery bars

⅓ c. butter or regular
  margarine
⅓ c. brown sugar, firmly
  packed
1 c. sifted flour
½ c. chopped walnuts

¼ c. sugar
1 (8 oz.) pkg. cream cheese
1 egg
2 tblsp. milk
1 tblsp. lemon juice
½ tsp. vanilla

Cream together butter and brown sugar until light and fluffy. Add flour and walnuts; mix well. Reserve ¾ c. mixture for topping. Press remaining mixture into greased 8″ square baking pan. Bake in 350° oven 12 to 15 minutes.

Beat together sugar and cream cheese until smooth. Beat in egg, milk, lemon juice and vanilla; mix well. Spread over baked crust. Sprinkle with reserved crumbs.

Bake in 350° oven 25 minutes or until done. Cool in pan on rack. Cut in 2″ squares. Makes 16 squares.

COFFEE-FLAVORED COOKIE SQUARES

Tuck these tender-crumbed cookies into packed lunches

½ c. butter or regular
  margarine
1 c. brown sugar, firmly
  packed
1 egg
1½ c. sifted flour
½ tsp. baking powder
½ tsp. baking soda

¼ tsp. salt
½ tsp. ground cinnamon
½ c. hot coffee
½ c. raisins
½ c. chopped walnuts
1 tblsp. flour
Thin Vanilla Glaze (recipe
  follows)

Cream together butter and sugar until light and fluffy. Add egg; beat well.

Sift together 1½ c. flour, baking powder, baking soda, salt and cinnamon. Add dry ingredients alternately with hot coffee to creamed mixture, mixing well after each addition.

Combine raisins, walnuts and 1 tblsp. flour; stir into dough. Spread in greased 13×9×2″ baking pan.

Bake in 350° oven 20 minutes or until done. Cool in pan on rack. While still warm, spread with Thin Vanilla Glaze. Cut in 2¼″ squares. Makes 2 dozen.

Thin Vanilla Glaze: Combine 1 c. sifted confectioners sugar, 1 tblsp. soft butter or regular margarine, 1 tsp. vanilla and 2½ tblsp. milk. Mix until smooth. Add more milk if necessary to make a thin glaze.

MAPLE WALNUT SQUARES

"Kansas sweepstakes winner . . . once Grandmother's recipe"

1½ c. sifted flour	1 c. maple-blended syrup
¼ c. brown sugar, firmly packed	2 eggs, slightly beaten
	½ tsp. vanilla
½ c. butter or regular margarine	2 tblsp. flour
	¼ tsp. salt
⅔ c. brown sugar, firmly packed	1 c. chopped walnuts

Combine 1½ c. flour and ¼ c. brown sugar. Cut in butter until mixture is crumbly. Press mixture into greased 13×9×2″ baking pan. Bake in 350° oven 15 minutes.

Combine ⅔ c. brown sugar and syrup in small saucepan; simmer 5 minutes. Slowly pour over eggs, stirring constantly. Stir in vanilla, 2 tblsp. flour and salt; mix thoroughly. Pour over baked crust. Sprinkle walnuts on top.

Bake in 350° oven 20 to 25 minutes or until done. Cool in pan on rack. Cut in 1¾″ squares. Makes about 2½ dozen.

COCONUT BAR COOKIES

A homemaker developed this recipe and won a Blue Ribbon

⅓ c. butter or regular
   margarine
1 c. sugar
2 eggs
1 tsp. vanilla

½ c. sifted flour
½ tsp. baking powder
½ tsp. salt
1 c. flaked coconut

Cream together butter and sugar until light and fluffy. Add eggs, one at a time, beating well after each addition. Add vanilla.

Sift together flour, baking powder and salt. Gradually add dry ingredients to creamed mixture; mixing well. Stir in coconut. Spread in greased and floured 8″ square baking pan.

Bake in 350° oven 30 minutes or until done. Cool in pan on rack. Cut in 2″ squares. Makes 16 squares.

GRAHAM CRACKER CHEWS

Cookies are even better after mellowing for 24 hours

1⅓ c. graham cracker
   crumbs
2 tblsp. flour
½ c. butter or regular
   margarine
2 eggs, well beaten
1 tsp. vanilla

⅓ c. graham cracker
   crumbs
1½ c. brown sugar, firmly
   packed
¼ tsp. baking powder
½ c. chopped walnuts

Combine 1⅓ c. graham cracker crumbs and flour. Cut in butter until mixture is crumbly. Press mixture into greased 9″ square baking pan. Bake in 350° oven 20 minutes.

Mix together eggs and vanilla.

Blend together ⅓ c. graham cracker crumbs, brown sugar, baking powder and walnuts; stir into eggs. Pour over baked crust.

Bake in 350° oven 20 minutes or until done. Cool in pan on rack. Cut in 3×1″ bars. Makes 27 bars.

TART LEMON SQUARES

A Grand Champion winner at a county fair in Wisconsin

1 c. sifted flour	½ tsp. baking powder
¼ c. confectioners sugar	⅛ tsp. salt
⅛ tsp. salt	2 eggs, slightly beaten
½ c. butter or regular	2 tblsp. lemon juice
margarine	1 tsp. grated lemon rind
1 c. sugar	Lemon Glaze (recipe
2 tblsp. flour	follows)

Combine 1 c. flour, confectioners sugar and ⅛ tsp. salt. Cut in butter until mixture is crumbly. Press mixture into greased 11×7×1½″ baking pan. Bake in 325° oven 15 minutes.

Combine sugar, 2 tblsp. flour, baking powder, ⅛ tsp. salt, eggs, lemon juice and lemon rind; mix thoroughly. Spread evenly over baked crust.

Bake in 325° oven 25 minutes. Cool in pan on rack. Spread with Lemon Glaze. Cut in 1¼″ squares. Makes 2½ dozen.

Lemon Glaze: Combine ½ c. sifted confectioners sugar, 1 tblsp. lemon juice, 1 tblsp. melted butter or regular margarine and 1 drop yellow food color. Blend until smooth.

PINEAPPLE OATMEAL BARS

Unusual pineapple bars that are rich and delicious

½ c. brown sugar, firmly	1 (1 lb. 4 oz.) can crushed
packed	pineapple, drained
1¼ c. quick-cooking oats	1 tblsp. cornstarch
½ c. sifted flour	½ c. sugar
¼ tsp. baking soda	½ c. light cream
¼ tsp. salt	1 egg yolk
½ c. butter or regular	
margarine	

Combine brown sugar, oats, flour, baking soda and salt. Cut in butter until mixture is crumbly. Press mixture into greased 11×7×1½″ baking dish.

Combine pineapple, cornstarch, sugar, light cream and egg yolk in saucepan. Cook until mixture is thick. Pour over crust.

Bake in 375° oven 30 minutes or until done. Cool in pan on rack. Cut in 2½ ×1¼″ bars. Makes 2 dozen.

DANISH APPLE BARS

A two-time winner of a Purple Ribbon in Nebraska

3 c. sifted flour	1 c. sugar
1 tsp. salt	1 tsp. ground cinnamon
1 c. shortening	1 egg white, beaten until
1 egg yolk, beaten	stiff
Milk	1 c. sifted confectioners
1 c. crushed corn flakes	sugar
8 large apples, pared and	3 tblsp. water
sliced (8 c.)	1 tsp. vanilla

Sift together flour and salt into bowl. Cut in shortening until crumbly. Add enough milk to egg yolk to make ½ c. Add to flour mixture; mix until moistened.

Divide dough almost in half. Roll out larger half; place in 15½ ×10½ ×1″ jelly roll pan. Press up on sides of pan. Sprinkle with corn flakes. Arrange apple slices over corn flakes. Combine sugar and cinnamon; sprinkle over apples. Roll out other half of dough to fit top. Make vents in top. Moisten edges of dough with water; seal. Spread egg white over crust.

Bake in 375° oven 1 hour or until golden.

Combine confectioners sugar, water and vanilla; mix well. Spread on bars while warm. Makes 12 servings.

OATMEAL DATE BARS

A 4-H fair winner in the Cookie Division in Maryland

3 c. cut-up dates	1 c. brown sugar, firmly
¼ c. sugar	packed
1 c. water	1¾ c. sifted flour
½ c. shortening	1 tsp. salt
¼ c. butter or regular	½ tsp. baking soda
margarine	1 c. quick-cooking oats

Combine dates, sugar and water in small saucepan. Cook over low heat, stirring constantly, until mixture is thick (about 10 minutes). Set aside to cool.

Cream together shortening, butter and brown sugar until light and fluffy.

Sift together flour, salt and baking soda. Gradually add dry ingredients to creamed mixture; mix well. Stir in oats. Press half of mixture in greased and floured 13×9×2″ baking pan. Spread with cooled date filling. Carefully top with remaining half of crumb mixture, patting lightly.

Bake in 400° oven 25 to 30 minutes or until done. Cool in pan on rack. Cut in 3×1½″ bars. Makes 2 dozen.

PRIZE BUTTER BARS

Serve these brown sugar-flavored bars for a coffee break

¾ c. butter
½ c. sugar
2 c. sifted flour
¼ tsp. salt
½ tsp. vanilla

¼ c. butter
1 (3 oz.) pkg. cream cheese
¾ c. brown sugar, firmly packed
1 c. chopped walnuts

Combine ¾ c. butter, sugar, flour, salt and vanilla. Beat at low speed on electric mixer until particles are fine. Set aside 1 c. mixture for topping. Press remaining mixture into ungreased 13×9×2″ baking pan.

Cream together ¼ c. butter, cream cheese and brown sugar until light and fluffy. Stir in walnuts. Spoon mixture over crumbs.

Bake in 375° oven 5 minutes. Remove from oven. Spread brown sugar mixture to cover crust. Sprinkle with reserved crumbs.

Bake 25 to 30 more minutes or until golden brown. Cool in pan on rack. Cut in 3×1½″ bars. Makes 21 bars.

SIX-LAYER COOKIES

Let cookies mellow overnight . . . easier to cut

½ c. butter or regular margarine

2 c. graham cracker crumbs

1⅓ c. flaked coconut

1 (6 oz.) pkg. semi-sweet chocolate pieces

1 (14 oz.) can sweetened condensed milk

1 c. chopped pecans

Melt butter in 13×9×2" baking pan over low heat. Remove from heat; sprinkle graham cracker crumbs evenly over melted butter. Then sprinkle with coconut and an even layer of chocolate pieces. Pour sweetened condensed milk evenly over layers. Top with nuts (do not stir).

Bake in 350° oven 35 minutes or until done. Cool in pan on rack. Cut in 2×1" bars. Makes 40 bars.

TOFFEE PECAN BARS

Rich, brown sugar-flavored bars won a Blue in a Missouri fair

1½ c. sifted flour

¾ c. brown sugar, firmly packed

¾ c. butter or regular margarine

2 eggs

1½ c. brown sugar, firmly packed

1½ tsp. vanilla

3 tblsp. flour

1½ tsp. baking powder

¾ tsp. salt

1⅓ c. flaked coconut

1½ c. chopped pecans

Combine 1½ c. flour and ¾ c. brown sugar in bowl. Cut in butter until mixture is crumbly. Press crumb mixture into greased 13×9×2" baking pan.

Bake in 350° oven 15 minutes.

Beat eggs well. Add 1½ c. brown sugar and vanilla; blend well. Combine 3 tblsp. flour, baking powder and salt. Stir dry ingredients into egg mixture; mix well. Stir in coconut and pecans. Spread topping over baked layer.

Bake in 350° oven 30 minutes or until topping is brown. Cool in pan on rack. While warm, cut in 3×1½" bars. Makes 2 dozen.

MARSHMALLOW FUDGE SQUARES

"My four brothers never tire of these," a Nebraska girl says

½ c. shortening	¼ tsp. baking powder
¾ c. sugar	¼ tsp. salt
2 eggs	½ c. chopped walnuts
1 tsp. vanilla	1 (7 oz.) jar marshmallow
¾ c. sifted flour	creme
2 tblsp. cocoa	

Cream together shortening and sugar until light and fluffy. Add eggs, one at a time, beating well after each addition. Blend in vanilla.

Sift together flour, cocoa, baking powder and salt. Add to creamed mixture, mixing well. Stir in walnuts. Spread in greased and floured 11×7×1½" baking pan.

Bake in 350° oven 30 minutes or until done. Immediately spread marshmallow creme evenly over top. Cool in pan on rack. Cut in 1¾" squares. Makes 28 squares.

SPICY APPLE SQUARES

A South Dakota teen-ager won a Purple Ribbon with these

⅔ c. butter or regular margarine	½ tsp. baking soda
1 c. sugar	½ tsp. ground nutmeg
2 eggs	¼ tsp. ground cloves
1 c. sifted flour	1 c. diced, pared apples
1 tsp. baking powder	¾ c. rolled oats
1 tsp. ground cinnamon	½ c. chopped walnuts
	Confectioners sugar

Cream together butter and sugar until light and fluffy. Add eggs, one at a time, beating well after each addition.

Sift together flour, baking powder, cinnamon, baking soda, nutmeg and cloves. Gradually add dry ingredients to creamed mixture; mix well. Stir in apples, oats and walnuts. Spread batter in greased 13×9×2″ cake pan.

Bake in 350° oven 25 to 30 minutes or until done. Cool in pan on rack. Sprinkle with confectioners sugar. Cut in 2¼″ squares. Makes 15.

PEANUT BUTTER BARS

Won the Sweepstakes in the Cookie Division in an Indiana fair

⅓ c. shortening
1 c. sugar
¼ c. brown sugar, firmly packed
½ c. peanut butter
2 eggs
1 tsp. vanilla
1 c. sifted flour

1 tsp. baking powder
¼ tsp. salt
1 (3½ oz.) can flaked coconut (1⅓ c.)
Confectioners Sugar Frosting (recipe follows)
Chopped Peanuts

Cream together shortening, sugars and peanut butter until light and fluffy. Add eggs, one at a time, beating well after each addition. Blend in vanilla.

Sift together flour, baking powder and salt. Add to creamed mixture, mixing thoroughly. Stir in coconut. Spread batter in greased 13×9×2″ baking pan.

Bake in 350° oven 25 minutes. Cool in pan on rack. Spread with Confectioners Sugar Frosting. Sprinkle with peanuts. Cut in 3×1½″ bars. Makes 2 dozen.

Confectioners Sugar Frosting: Combine 2 c. sifted confectioners sugar, ¼ c. soft butter or regular margarine, 1 tsp. vanilla, ¼ tsp. salt and 3 tblsp. light cream; beat until smooth.

HEIRLOOM COOKIES FOR THE HOLIDAYS

"I found my Molasses Crinkles in one of my mother's very old cookbooks and it has won both a Blue and Purple Ribbon at the Missouri State Fair," says a farm wife and mother adding "My children always expect to find a big cookie jar filled with 'Crinkles' when they visit Grandma at Christmastime and she never disappoints them."

"It wouldn't be Christmas on our Minnesota farm without a big plateful of Rich Butterscotch Cookies. I wrap the rich buttery dough around a pecan or walnut half and then roll the baked cookie in confectioners sugar. They freeze well and keep indefinitely. The recipe has been in our family for years."

"The recipe for German Spice Cookies has been made for years by both my grandmother and great-grandmother," said a homemaker from Iowa. "In fact when my grandmother visited relatives in Germany last year she discovered that they also still make these spicy molasses cookies at Christmastime." This fair winner is extra spicy, crackled on the top, crunchy on the outside and moist and chewy inside.

You will want to bake these heirloom winners—they truly are great cookie treasures.

MOLASSES CRINKLES

"Fourteen children look forward to these at Grandmother's"

¼ c. shortening	2¼ c. sifted flour
½ c. butter or regular margarine	2 tsp. baking soda
	1 tsp. ground ginger
1 c. brown sugar, firmly packed	½ tsp. ground cloves
	¼ tsp. salt
1 egg	Sugar
¼ c. molasses	

Cream together shortening, butter and brown sugar until light and fluffy. Add egg and molasses; blend well.

Sift together flour, baking soda, ginger, cloves and salt. Gradually add dry ingredients to creamed mixture; mix well. Chill dough in refrigerator 1 hour.

Shape dough in balls the size of a large walnut. Dip tops in sugar. Place balls sugared side up about 3″ apart on greased baking sheets.

Bake in 375° oven 10 to 12 minutes or until done. Remove from baking sheets; cool on racks. Makes about 4 dozen.

RICH BUTTERSCOTCH COOKIES

Roll balls of dough in coconut or chopped nuts before baking

2 c. butter or regular
   margarine
1 c. plus 2 tblsp. brown
   sugar, firmly packed

1½ tsp. vanilla
4 c. sifted flour
½ tsp. salt

Cream together butter and brown sugar until light and fluffy. Blend in vanilla.

Sift together flour and salt. Gradually add dry ingredients; mix well. Chill dough in refrigerator 2 hours.

Shape dough in 1″ balls. Place balls about 2″ apart on greased baking sheets. Flatten slightly with bottom of drinking glass dipped in sugar.

Bake in 350° oven 12 minutes or until golden brown. Remove from baking sheets; cool on racks. Makes 8 dozen.

GERMAN SPICE COOKIES

Heirloom cookie recipe originally from Germany

1 c. shortening
2 c. brown sugar, firmly
   packed
3 eggs
⅔ c. molasses
1 tsp. vanilla
6½ c. sifted flour

2 tsp. ground cinnamon
1 tsp. baking soda
1 tsp. ground ginger
1 tsp. ground cloves
½ tsp. salt
⅓ c. sour milk

Cream together shortening and brown sugar until light and fluffy. Add eggs, one at a time, beating well after each addition. Beat in molasses and vanilla.

Sift together flour, cinnamon, baking soda, ginger, cloves and salt. Add dry ingredients alternately with sour milk to creamed mixture, beating well after each addition. Chill dough in refrigerator 1 hour.

Shape dough in balls the size of a walnut. Place balls about 2" apart on greased baking sheets.

Bake in 350° oven 15 minutes or until golden brown. Remove from baking sheets; cool on racks. Makes 8 dozen.

WINNING SUGAR COOKIES

Rich, buttery sugar cookies that melt in your mouth

1 c. butter or regular margarine	1 c. cooking oil
1 c. sugar	1 tsp. vanilla
1 c. sifted confectioners sugar	4 c. sifted flour
2 eggs	1 tsp. baking soda
	1 tsp. cream of tartar
	½ tsp. salt

Cream together butter and sugars until light and fluffy. Add eggs, one at a time, beating well after each addition. Blend in oil and vanilla.

Sift together flour, baking soda, cream of tartar and salt. Gradually add dry ingredients to creamed mixture; mix well. Chill dough in refrigerator 8 hours or overnight.

Shape dough in balls the size of a walnut. Place balls about 2" apart on ungreased baking sheets.

Bake in 350° oven 10 to 12 minutes or until done. Remove from baking sheets; cool on racks. Makes about 7 dozen.

NO-ROLL SUGAR COOKIES

Golden, crunchy sugar cookies with crackled sugar tops

1 c. butter or regular margarine	1 tsp. cream of tartar
2 c. sugar	1 tsp. baking soda
2 eggs	1 tsp. salt
1 tsp. vanilla	Sugar
3 c. sifted flour	Water

Cream together butter and 2 c. sugar until light and fluffy. Add eggs, one at a time, beating well after each addition. Add vanilla.

Sift together flour, cream of tartar, baking soda and salt. Gradually add to creamed mixture; mix well. Chill dough in refrigerator 1 hour.

Shape dough in 1" balls; dip in sugar. Place balls about 2" apart on greased baking sheets. Make a slight indentation in each cookie; drop 2 to 3 drops water in each.

Bake in 350° oven about 20 minutes or until golden brown. Remove from baking sheets; cool on racks. Makes 4 dozen.

LEMON/CHEESE COOKIES

Delicate, subtle lemon-flavored cookie that is so unusual

½ c. butter or regular margarine
1 (3 oz.) pkg. cream cheese
½ c. sugar
1 tsp. grated lemon rind
¼ tsp. lemon extract

1 c. sifted flour
2 tsp. baking powder
¼ tsp. salt
1¼ c. coarsely crumbled corn flakes

Cream together butter, cream cheese and sugar until light and fluffy. Blend in lemon rind and lemon extract.

Sift together flour, baking powder and salt. Gradually add dry ingredients to creamed mixture; mix well. Chill dough in refrigerator about 1 hour.

Shape dough in 1" balls. Roll each in corn flake crumbs. Place balls about 2" apart on ungreased baking sheets.

Bake in 350° oven 12 to 15 minutes or until done. Remove from baking sheets; cool on racks. Makes about 3 dozen.

CINNAMON SUGAR COOKIES

Old favorite recipe that has passed from hand to hand

½ c. shortening	2 tsp. cream of tartar
½ c. butter or regular margarine	1 tsp. baking soda
	¼ tsp. salt
1½ c. sugar	2 tblsp. sugar
2 eggs	1 tblsp. ground cinnamon
1 tsp. vanilla	
2¾ c. plus 2 tblsp. sifted flour	

Cream together shortening, butter and 1½ c. sugar until light and fluffy. Add eggs, one at a time, beating well after each addition. Blend in vanilla.

Sift together flour, cream of tartar, baking soda and salt. Gradually add dry ingredients to creamed mixture; mix well. Chill in refrigerator 1 hour.

Combine 2 tblsp. sugar and cinnamon.

Shape dough into balls the size of a walnut. Roll each in sugar-cinnamon mixture. Place balls about 2″ apart on greased baking sheets.

Bake in 350° oven 12 to 15 minutes or until done. Remove from baking sheets; cool on racks. Makes about 5 dozen.

SWEDISH BUTTER NUT COOKIES

Attractive cookies to serve at your next bridal shower

2 c. butter or regular margarine	1 tsp. almond extract
	4½ c. flour
1½ c. sugar	1 egg white, slightly beaten
6 egg yolks	1 c. ground walnuts

Cream together butter and sugar until light and fluffy. Blend in egg yolks and almond extract. Gradually add flour to creamed mixture; mix well.

Shape dough in 2″ strips about ½″ thick. Dip in egg white,

then in walnuts. Place about 2″ apart on ungreased baking sheets.

Bake in 425° oven 8 to 10 minutes or until golden brown. Remove from baking sheets; cool on racks. Makes 12 dozen.

DELICIOUS CHOCOLATE COOKIES

Blue Ribbon winner says these are always a favorite

½ c. butter or regular margarine	4 eggs
4 (1 oz.) squares unsweetened chocolate	2 c. sifted flour
	2 tsp. baking powder
2 c. sugar	¼ tsp. salt
2 tsp. vanilla	½ c. chopped walnuts
	Confectioners sugar

Melt together butter and chocolate over low heat. Combine chocolate mixture, sugar and vanilla; blend well. Add eggs, one at a time, beating well after each addition.

Sift together flour, baking powder and salt. Gradually add dry ingredients to creamed mixture; mix well. Stir in walnuts. Chill dough in refrigerator several hours.

Shape dough in 1″ balls. Roll in confectioners sugar. Place balls about 2″ apart on greased baking sheets.

Bake in 350° oven 15 minutes or until done. Remove from baking sheets. Cool on racks. Makes 6 dozen.

GREAT GIFT ASSORTMENT

One of the most thoughtful and most appreciated gifts that you can give is a box of homemade cookies. Especially if they are Blue Ribbon winners!

Once you have browsed through these recipes, you will want to make a batch of each one and mix and match your gift assortment.

Tiny and delicate, Mint Chip Meringues are pretty as well as delicious. The Holiday Fruit Drops, chock-full of candied fruit, won the Mayor's Cookie Plate as well as several Blue Ribbons at the Kansas State Fair. A soft drop cookie, Date Pecan Cookies, is a Blue Ribbon winner from the Tennessee State Fair, and the crunchy Brown Sugar Cookies is a two-time Blue Ribbon winner from Idaho.

MINT CHIP MERINGUES

Cool mint-flavored meringues that melt in your mouth

2 egg whites
¾ tsp. cream of tartar
¼ tsp. salt
¾ c. sugar

1 (6 oz.) pkg. semi-sweet
    mint chocolate pieces
4 drops green food color

Beat egg whites, cream of tartar and salt until soft peaks form. Gradually add sugar, beating until stiff peaks form. Fold in mint chocolate pieces and food color. Drop by teaspoonfuls about 2" apart on waxed-paper-lined baking sheets.

Place in 350° oven and turn off heat. Leave meringues in oven at least 12 hours. Makes 2½ dozen.

HOLIDAY FRUIT DROPS

A colorful addition to the holiday cookie plate

½ c. shortening
½ c. butter or regular
    margarine
2 c. brown sugar, firmly
    packed
2 eggs
3½ c. sifted flour

1 tsp. baking soda
1 tsp. salt
½ c. water
1½ c. chopped walnuts
2 c. mixed candied fruit
½ c. halved, candied red
    cherries

Cream together shortening, butter and brown sugar until light and fluffy. Add eggs, one at a time, beating well after each addition.

Sift together flour, baking soda and salt. Add dry ingredients alternately with water to creamed mixture, mixing well after each addition. Stir in walnuts, candied fruit and cherries. Chill dough in refrigerator 1 hour.

Drop by teaspoonfuls on greased baking sheets.

Bake in 400° oven 8 to 10 minutes or until done. Remove from baking sheets; cool on racks. Makes 7½ dozen.

DATE PECAN COOKIES

These attractive soft cookies are great for the holidays

1 c. shortening
2 c. brown sugar, firmly packed
2 eggs
3½ c. sifted flour
1 tsp. baking soda
1 tsp. salt

½ c. buttermilk
1½ c. chopped pecans
2 c. halved, candied red cherries
2 c. cut-up dates
Pecan halves

Cream together shortening and brown sugar until light and fluffy. Add eggs, one at a time, beating well after each addition.

Sift together flour, baking soda and salt. Add dry ingredients alternately with buttermilk, beating well after each addition. Stir in pecans, cherries and dates. Chill dough in refrigerator 1 hour.

Drop by teaspoonfuls about 2" apart on greased baking sheets. Place a pecan half on each cookie.

Bake in 375° oven 10 minutes or until done. Remove from baking sheets; cool on racks. Makes 6 dozen.

BROWN SUGAR COOKIES

Crunchy cookies with real butterscotch flavor

1½ c. shortening
1½ c. brown sugar, firmly packed
2 eggs
2 tsp. vanilla
2½ c. sifted flour

1 tsp. baking soda
½ tsp. cream of tartar
½ c. chopped walnuts
1 (6 oz.) pkg. semi-sweet chocolate pieces

Cream together shortening and brown sugar until light and fluffy. Add eggs, one at a time, beating well after each addition. Blend in vanilla.

Sift together flour, baking soda and cream of tartar. Gradually add dry ingredients to creamed mixture, mixing well. Stir in walnuts and chocolate pieces. Drop by teaspoonfuls about 2" apart on greased baking sheet.

Bake in 350° oven 8 to 10 minutes or until done. Remove from baking sheets; cool on racks. Makes about 5 dozen.

CRISP OATMEAL COOKIES

The brown sugar flavor makes these cookies a favorite

1 c. butter or regular margarine	1½ c. sifted flour
1 c. brown sugar, firmly packed	1 tsp. baking powder
	1 tsp. baking soda
1 c. sugar	2 c. quick-cooking oats
2 eggs	1 c. flaked coconut
2 tsp. vanilla	2½ c. oven-toasted rice cereal

Cream together butter and sugars until fluffy. Add eggs, one at a time, beating well after each addition. Blend in vanilla.

Sift together flour, baking powder and baking soda. Gradually add dry ingredients to creamed mixture; mixing well. Stir in oats, coconut and rice cereal. Drop by teaspoonfuls about 2" apart on greased baking sheets.

Bake in 325° oven 12 to 15 minutes or until done. Cool slightly on baking sheets. Remove from baking sheets; cool on racks. Makes about 5½ dozen.

GOLDEN CARROT COOKIES

These attractive cookies are perfect with iced tea

¾ c. butter or regular margarine	½ tsp. lemon extract
	2 c. sifted flour
¾ c. sugar	2 tsp. baking powder
1 egg	½ tsp. salt
1 tsp. vanilla	1¼ c. grated, pared carrots

Cream together butter and sugar until light and fluffy. Add egg; beat well. Blend in vanilla and lemon extract.

Sift together flour, baking powder and salt. Gradually add dry ingredients to creamed mixture; mix well. Stir in carrots. Drop by teaspoonfuls about 2" apart on greased baking sheets.

Bake in 375° oven 15 minutes or until done. Remove from baking sheets; cool on racks. Makes 4 dozen.

DROP SUGAR COOKIES

Delicate buttery cookies sure to please the family

½ c. butter or regular margarine	1¾ c. sifted flour
	½ tsp. baking powder
1 c. sugar	½ tsp. baking soda
1 egg	¼ c. milk
1 tsp. vanilla	½ c. chopped walnuts

Cream together butter and sugar until light and fluffy. Add egg; beat well. Blend in vanilla.

Sift together flour, baking powder and baking soda. Add dry ingredients alternately with milk, beating well after each addition. Stir in walnuts. Drop by teaspoonfuls about 2" apart on greased baking sheets. Flatten with back of spoon.

Bake in 375° oven 8 to 10 minutes or until done. Remove from baking sheets; cool on racks. Makes about 2½ dozen.

APPLESAUCE RAISIN COOKIES

These cookies were rated "excellent" in a New Jersey 4-H fair

½ c. shortening	½ tsp. salt
1 c. sugar	½ tsp. ground cinnamon
1 egg	¼ tsp. ground cloves
1 c. applesauce	½ c. raisins
2½ c. sifted flour	½ c. chopped walnuts
1 tsp. baking powder	1 tblsp. flour
½ tsp. baking soda	Confectioners sugar

Cream together shortening and sugar until light and fluffy. Add egg and applesauce; blend well.

Sift together 2½ c. flour, baking powder, baking soda, salt, cinnamon and cloves. Gradually add dry ingredients to creamed mixture; mix well. Combine raisins, walnuts and 1 tblsp. flour. Stir into dough. Drop by teaspoonfuls about 2" apart on greased baking sheets.

Bake in 375° oven 12 minutes or until golden brown. Remove from baking sheets. Cool on racks. Roll in confectioners sugar. Makes 4 dozen.

THE FAMILY COOKIE JAR

The family's enthusiasm for a certain homemade cookie often prompts a homemaker to enter it in a fair exhibit. Certainly, she's had enough experience baking them to have achieved perfection.

"My recipe for Ranger Oatmeal Cookies has won several Blues at a Louisiana fair," says a prize winner. "When my daughter was growing up I always kept the cookie jar full of these cookies."

Golden brown and chewy with a pretty cracked top, these Purple Ribbon Cracked Coconut Oat Cookies look and taste like macaroons.

Chewy Honey Cookies, a soft old-fashioned cookie from a Minnesota farm wife, won a Blue at the fair. She makes big fat cookies for the family and a smaller version to serve to guests.

RANGER OATMEAL COOKIES

A Louisiana woman has won several ribbons with this recipe

1 c. shortening	1½ tsp. baking soda
1 c. sugar	1 tsp. baking powder
1 c. brown sugar, firmly packed	½ tsp. salt
	1 c. quick-cooking oats
2 eggs	1 c. chopped walnuts
1 tsp. vanilla	1 c. flaked coconut
2 c. sifted flour	1 c. oven-toasted rice cereal

Cream together shortening and sugars until light and fluffy. Add eggs, one at a time, beating well after each addition. Beat in vanilla.

Sift together flour, baking soda, baking powder and salt. Gradually add dry ingredients to creamed mixture; mix well. Stir in oats, walnuts, coconut and rice cereal. Shape into 1" balls. Place balls about 2" apart on greased baking sheets.

Bake in 350° oven 15 minutes or until done. Remove from baking sheets. Cool on racks. Makes 6 dozen.

CRACKED COCONUT OAT COOKIES

Recipe was developed by a 4-H member and became a winner

1 c. shortening	2 c. sifted flour
1 c. brown sugar, firmly packed	1 tsp. baking powder
	1 tsp. baking soda
1 c. sugar	½ tsp. salt
2 eggs	2 c. quick-cooking oats
2 tsp. vanilla	1 c. flaked coconut

Cream together shortening and sugars until light and fluffy. Add eggs, one at a time, beating well after each addition. Blend in vanilla.

Sift together flour, baking powder, baking soda and salt. Gradually add dry ingredients to creamed mixture; mix well. Stir in oats and coconut. (Dough is very stiff.) Shape dough in 1" balls. Place balls about 2" apart on greased baking sheets. Flatten each with bottom of drinking glass dipped in water.

Bake in 350° oven about 15 minutes or until golden brown. Remove from baking sheets; cool on racks. Makes 7 dozen.

CHEWY HONEY COOKIES

Make large cookies for family lunch boxes and picnics

1½ c. shortening	2 tsp. vanilla
2 c. sugar	4½ c. sifted flour
½ c. honey	4 tsp. baking soda
2 eggs	½ tsp. salt

Cream together shortening and sugar until light and fluffy. Blend in honey. Add eggs, one at a time, beating well after each addition. Blend in vanilla.

Sift together flour, baking soda and salt. Gradually add dry ingredients to creamed mixture; mix well. Shape dough in 1" balls. Place balls about 2" apart on greased baking sheets. Flatten slightly with bottom of drinking glass dipped in flour.

Bake in 350° oven 12 to 15 minutes or until golden brown. Remove from baking sheets; cool on racks. Makes about 7 dozen.

MOM'S GINGERSNAPS

Everyone in our Test Kitchens agreed that these were winners

¾ c. shortening	1 tsp. salt
1 c. sugar	1 tsp. ground ginger
1 egg	½ tsp. ground cinnamon
¼ c. molasses	¼ tsp. ground cloves
2¼ c. sifted flour	1½ c. raisins
2 tsp. baking soda	3 tblsp. sugar

Cream together shortening and sugar until light and fluffy. Blend in egg and molasses.

Sift together flour, baking soda, salt, ginger, cinnamon and cloves. Gradually add dry ingredients to creamed mixture; mix well. Stir in raisins. Chill dough in refrigerator 8 hours or overnight.

Shape dough in 1¼" balls. Roll in 3 tblsp. sugar. Place balls about 2" apart on greased baking sheets.

Bake in 375° oven 12 minutes or until surface is crackled. Cool 2 minutes on baking sheets. Remove from baking sheets; cool on racks. Makes about 4 dozen.

SPICY MOLASSES COOKIES

Always a favorite, old-fashioned chewy spice cookies

1½ c. melted shortening	2 tsp. ground cinnamon
2 c. sugar	1 tsp. salt
2 eggs	1 tsp. ground cloves
½ c. molasses	1 tsp. ground ginger
4 c. sifted flour	Sugar
4 tsp. baking soda	

Combine melted shortening and 2 c. sugar; beat until blended. Add eggs, one at a time, beating well after each addition. Gradually stir in molasses.

Stir together flour, baking soda, cinnamon, salt, cloves and ginger. Gradually add dry ingredients to molasses mixture; mix well. Chill dough in refrigerator 8 hours or overnight.

Shape dough in balls the size of a walnut. Roll each in sugar. Place balls about 2″ apart on ungreased baking sheets.

Bake in 375° oven 8 to 10 minutes or until done. Let cool slightly on baking sheets. Remove from baking sheets; cool on racks. Makes about 7 dozen.

OATMEAL COOKIES

You can't stop with just one of these chewy cookies

1 c. shortening	2 c. sifted flour
1 c. brown sugar, firmly packed	1 tsp. baking powder
1 c. sugar	1 tsp. baking soda
2 eggs	1 tsp. salt
1 tsp. vanilla	1½ c. quick-cooking oats
	1 c. flaked coconut

Cream together shortening and sugars until light and fluffy. Add eggs, one at a time, beating well after each addition. Blend in vanilla.

Sift together flour, baking powder, baking soda and salt. Gradually add dry ingredients to creamed mixture; mix well. Stir in oats and coconut. Shape dough in small balls. Place balls about 2" apart on greased baking sheets.

Bake in 350° oven 10 to 12 minutes or until golden brown. Remove from baking sheets; cool on racks. Makes about 5 dozen.

CRUNCHY PEANUT BUTTER COOKIES

Always popular with children for after-school snacks

½ c. shortening	½ c. crunchy peanut butter
½ c. sugar	1 tsp. vanilla
½ c. brown sugar, firmly packed	2 c. sifted flour
	½ tsp. baking soda
1 egg	½ tsp. salt

Cream together shortening and sugars until light and fluffy. Beat in egg and peanut butter. Blend in vanilla.

Sift together flour, baking soda and salt. Gradually add dry ingredients to creamed mixture; blend well. Shape dough in 1" balls. Place balls about 2" apart on greased baking sheets. Flatten with floured tines of a fork.

Bake in 375° oven 8 to 10 minutes or until golden brown. Remove from baking sheets; cool on racks. Makes about 4 dozen.

PEANUT BUTTER COOKIES

A young Wisconsin girl won a Blue Ribbon with these cookies

1 c. shortening	1 c. peanut butter
1 c. sugar	1 tsp. vanilla
1 c. brown sugar, firmly packed	3 c. sifted flour
	1½ tsp. baking soda
2 eggs	½ tsp. salt

Cream together shortening and sugars until light and fluffy. Beat in eggs, one at a time, beating well after each addition. Beat in peanut butter and vanilla; blend well.

Sift together flour, baking soda and salt. Gradually add dry ingredients to creamed mixture; mix well. Shape into 1" balls.

Place balls about 2″ apart on greased baking sheets. Flatten with floured tines of a fork.

Bake in 400° oven 12 minutes or until golden brown. Remove from baking sheets. Cool on racks. Makes about 5½ dozen.

COCONUT OATMEAL COOKIES

A much asked-for cookie in one family for over 20 years

1 c. melted shortening
1 c. brown sugar, firmly
  packed
1 c. sugar
2 eggs
1 tsp. vanilla

1 c. sifted flour
1 tsp. baking soda
¼ tsp. salt
1 c. flaked coconut
2 c. quick-cooking oats

Combine shortening and sugars; beat until light and fluffy. Add eggs, one at a time, beating well after each addition. Blend in vanilla.

Sift together flour, baking soda and salt. Gradually add dry ingredients to creamed mixture; mix well. Stir in coconut and oats. Shape dough in 1″ balls. Place balls about 2″ apart on greased baking sheets.

Bake in 325° oven 12 minutes or until golden brown. Remove from baking sheets; cool on racks. Makes 6 dozen.

Chapter 4

HOMEMADE PIES THAT DESERVE THEIR RIBBONS

Good cooks have been taking pride in their homemade pies since the early pioneer days. And as we visited fairs cross-country we realized that there are a great many cooks today who can turn out a tender flaky crust with superb filling.

Hundreds of pies were on display, cherry, apple, pecan, mincemeat—each one a bit different—and all delicious. The apple pies varied in amount of spices and in the cut of the apple. Some were sliced, some diced—others cut into fat chunks. Some of the cherry pies were faintly flavored with almond, some with a quick grating of orange rind and others had a tart lemony taste mingled with the cherries.

We sampled enough pecan pies to last us through several Thanksgivings. Again they varied according to the cook's treasured recipe. Some women always finely chop their pecans, others break them into large pieces and some prefer to use the jumbo-sized pecans and leave them whole.

The meringue pies were something to behold—high fluffs with soft brown peaks and fillings with a perfect set . . . a delicate quiver when placed on the plate.

Some pies were latticed with bright fruit fillings peeking through. Others were crusty and glistening with sugar. Some edges were crimped, some fluted, some scalloped. Some fair competitors went a creative step further and cut hearts, crescents, diamonds and stars from pastry to decorate an open-faced pie.

A rich tender, flaky crust is the secret of a perfect pie. Many cooks feel that while they might be experts in baking cakes, breads and cookies, they just don't have a "knack" with pie crust. However, if all the techniques are mastered, with practice and tender handling of the dough, everyone can turn out a superb pie crust every time.

How to Judge a Perfect Pie Crust

A perfect pie crust is golden brown, with a blistery surface, brown undercrust. It's tender, flaky and crisp, fits well in the pan and has an attractive well-formed edge. It cuts easily, holding its shape when placed on a serving plate.

COMMON PROBLEMS WITH PIE CRUST . . . AND PROBABLE CAUSES

Tough crust—insufficient fat, too much water, overmixing or too much flour on board.

Crumbly crust—too little water, too much fat or undermixing.

Pale crust—too little fat, too much water, too much flour on board, overmixing, rolled too thick or too low an oven temperature.

Soggy lower crust—filling too moist, bottom crust torn or broken, soaked before baking starts, too low baking temperature or too short a baking period.

Shrinkage—unbalanced recipe, too much handling, pastry stretched too tightly in the pan, overchilled dough or dough uneven in thickness.

Dry mealy pastry—shortening was cut in too fine or too little water added.

Uneven edge—crust not rolled in even circle or not carefully shaped.

Large air bubbles—insufficient pricking.

TIPS TO HELP YOU BAKE A PERFECT PIE CRUST

Measure all ingredients accurately. Too much or too little flour, shortening or water can produce an unsatisfactory result.

Use a light touch. Too much handling toughens pastry.

For a glistening, extra-flaky top crust in fruit pies, brush with milk or cream, then sprinkle with sugar.

TIPS TO HELP YOU MAKE A PERFECT MERINGUE

To prevent shrinkage and weeping of meringue (a liquid film between pie filling and meringue), spread meringue carefully over surface of slightly cooled filling. Make sure that it is sealed to the crust.

To prevent beading (amber sugar drops on surface of meringue) the sugar must be thoroughly dissolved in the egg whites. Beat egg whites only until *frothy*, then very gradually beat in the sugar, beating well after each addition.

AWARD-WINNING APPLE PIES

Farm women know how to turn out some of the best apple pies in the world. We've chosen some of the most outstanding ones at country fairs. Of course we have a Basic Apple Pie that is piled high with apples and spiced just right. But we also have interesting variations of the basic apple: for example, a Whole Wheat Apple Pie made with whole wheat flour, cinnamon and sour cream, developed by a Minnesota farm wife as a solution to her husband's special diet—and he liked it better than a plain apple pie. The judges approved too; they gave her a Blue Ribbon.

Plan on seconds when you serve Crumb-topped Apple Pecan Pie—trickling with juices, scented with cinnamon and nutmeg, this Oklahoma Ribbon recipe originated in Chelsea, England.

BASIC APPLE PIE

Top with scoops of vanilla ice cream dusted with cinnamon

6 c. thinly sliced, peeled apples	**½ tsp. ground cinnamon**
	½ tsp. ground nutmeg
1 c. sugar	**Pastry for 2-crust 9″ pie**
1 tblsp. cornstarch	

Combine apples, sugar, cornstarch, cinnamon and nutmeg. Arrange apple mixture in pastry-lined pie plate.

Roll out remaining pastry; cut in ½″ strips. Interlace strips in crisscross fashion over filling to make lattice top. Trim strips even with pie edge. Turn bottom crust up over ends of strips. Press firmly to seal edge. Flute edge.

Bake in 400° oven 45 minutes or until apples are tender. Cool on rack. Makes 6 to 8 servings.

WHOLE WHEAT APPLE PIE

Unusual and so good. You'll want to serve this often

6 c. thinly sliced, peeled apples	1 c. whole wheat flour
⅔ c. sugar	½ c. brown sugar, firmly packed
2 tblsp. whole wheat flour	½ c. soft butter or regular margarine
1 tsp. ground cinnamon	½ tsp. ground cinnamon
½ c. dairy sour cream	
1 tsp. vanilla	
Whole Wheat Pie Shell (recipe follows)	

Combine apples, sugar, 2 tblsp. whole wheat flour, 1 tsp. cinnamon, sour cream and vanilla; mix well. Spoon into Whole Wheat Pie Shell.

Combine 1 c. whole wheat flour, brown sugar, butter and ½ tsp. cinnamon; mix until crumbly. Sprinkle over top of pie.

Bake in 350° oven 1 hour or until topping is golden brown and apples are tender. Cool on rack. Makes 6 to 8 servings.

Whole Wheat Pie Shell: Combine 1¼ c. whole wheat flour, 2 tsp. sugar, 1 tsp. salt, ½ c. cooking oil and 2 tblsp. milk; mix well. Press mixture evenly into 9″ pie plate.

CRUMB-TOPPED APPLE PECAN PIE

If the apples you use are sweet, reduce sugar to ½ cup

6 c. sliced, peeled tart
   apples
¼ c. chopped pecans
1 c. sugar
2 tsp. flour
¾ tsp. ground cinnamon

¼ tsp. ground nutmeg
1 unbaked 9" fluted pie
   shell
Crumb Topping (recipe
   follows)

Combine apples, pecans, sugar, flour, cinnamon and nutmeg. Arrange apple mixture in pie shell. Sprinkle with Crumb Topping.

Bake in 425° oven 10 minutes. Reduce heat to 350° and bake 35 minutes or until apples are tender. Cool on rack. Makes 6 to 8 servings.

Crumb Topping: Combine ½ c. brown sugar, firmly packed, ⅓ c. flour, ¼ c. soft butter or regular margarine, ¼ c. chopped pecans and ¼ tsp. ground cinnamon; mix until crumbly.

SPICY APPLE PIE

Serve pie slightly warm with a wedge of aged Cheddar

6 c. sliced, peeled apples
1 c. sugar
¼ c. flour
1 tsp. ground cinnamon

½ tsp. ground nutmeg
Pastry for 2-crust 9" pie
3 tblsp. butter or regular
   margarine

Combine apples, sugar, flour, cinnamon and nutmeg; mix well. Arrange in pastry-lined pie plate. Dot with butter. Adjust top crust and flute edge; cut vents.

Bake in 400° oven 45 minutes or until apples are tender. Cool on rack. Makes 6 to 8 servings.

APPLE CRUNCH PIE

Take this luscious pie to the next family reunion

9 c. thinly sliced, peeled
   apples
½ c. sugar
½ tsp. ground cinnamon
⅓ c. orange juice
1 unbaked 9″ pie shell
½ c. quick-cooking oats

½ c. flour
⅓ c. brown sugar, firmly
   packed
3 tblsp. melted butter or
   regular margarine
½ tsp. ground cinnamon

Combine apples, sugar, ½ tsp. cinnamon and orange juice; mix well. Arrange in pie shell.

Mix together oats, flour, brown sugar, butter and ½ tsp. cinnamon until crumbly. Sprinkle over apples.

Bake in 425° oven 10 minutes. Reduce heat to 350° and bake 55 minutes or until apples are tender. Cool on rack. Makes 6 to 8 servings.

SOUR CREAM APPLE PIE

If you store this pie overnight, be sure to refrigerate it

2 tblsp. flour
¼ tsp. salt
¾ c. sugar
¼ tsp. ground nutmeg
1 egg
1 c. dairy sour cream
1 tsp. vanilla

3 c. diced, peeled apples
1 unbaked 9″ pie shell
⅓ c. sugar
⅓ c. flour
1 tsp. ground cinnamon
2 tblsp. butter or regular
   margarine

Sift together 2 tblsp. flour, salt, ¾ c. sugar and nutmeg into bowl. Combine egg, sour cream and vanilla. Add to dry ingredients; mix well. Stir in apples. Spoon into pie shell.

Bake in 400° oven 15 minutes. Reduce heat to 350° and continue baking 30 minutes.

Combine ⅓ c. sugar, ⅓ c. flour, cinnamon and butter. Mix until crumbly. Remove pie from oven. Increase oven to 400°.

Sprinkle topping over filling. Return pie to oven and bake 10 minutes more. Cool on rack. Makes 6 to 8 servings.

CUSTARD APPLE TART

An elegant dessert that is surprisingly easy to make

2 c. sifted flour	6 c. sliced, pared apples
½ tsp. salt	¼ c. butter or regular
⅔ c. shortening	margarine
6 tblsp. water	4 eggs
⅔ c. dry bread crumbs	1½ c. heavy cream
½ tsp. sugar	½ c. sugar
2 tsp. ground cinnamon	½ tsp. ground nutmeg
½ tsp. salt	⅔ c. apple jelly

Sift together flour and ½ tsp. salt into bowl. Cut in shortening until crumbly. Sprinkle water over surface; stir until moistened. Shape into ball.

Divide dough in half. Roll out on lightly floured surface to a 12″ circle. Line 10″ flan pan with dough. Repeat with remaining dough. Combine bread crumbs, ½ tsp. sugar, cinnamon and ½ tsp. salt. Sprinkle half of bread crumb mixture in bottom of each pan. Arrange apple slices in a swirl pattern over crumbs, overlapping slices. Dot with butter.

Bake in 425° oven 15 minutes.

Beat eggs well. Stir in heavy cream, ½ c. sugar and nutmeg. Pour over apples in each pan. Reduce heat to 375°; bake 25 minutes or until custard is set and apples are tender.

Heat apple jelly in saucepan over low heat; stir until smooth. Spoon over hot tarts. Cool in pans on racks. Makes 2 tarts.

PLUMP AND JUICY FRUIT PIES

Take your pick of this marvelous variety of fruit pies. If your family prefers a pie that's a bit on the tart side, try Apricot Lattice Pie, an Oklahoma State Fair Champion. It's tart but with an underlying sweetness. "I experimented with my recipe for

Easy Mincemeat Pie until I had the flavor and texture just right—it really does taste like 'homemade' mincemeat and I've won a number of Blues," another Oklahoma woman told us. It does have a delightful balance of spices and a refreshing hint of lemon.

The sparkling ruby red Cranberry Raspberry Pie has won a half-dozen Blue Ribbons so far. The South Dakota winner always makes this at Christmas—the almond pie crust adds a special flavor.

APRICOT LATTICE PIE

A State Fair Champion in pie baking sent this recipe

2 (8 oz.) pkgs. dried apricots	2 tblsp. soft butter or regular margarine
Water	1 tblsp. lemon juice
1¼ c. sugar	Pastry for 2-crust 9″ pie
¼ tsp. salt	Milk
¼ tsp. ground nutmeg	Sugar
¼ tsp. ground cinnamon	
2½ tblsp. quick-cooking tapioca	

Place apricots in 3-qt. saucepan. Add enough water to cover. Bring to a boil, reduce heat and simmer until apricots are tender (about 25 minutes). Remove from heat. Drain apricots, reserving 1¼ c. liquid. Cool.

Combine 1¼ c. sugar, salt, nutmeg, cinnamon, tapioca, butter and lemon juice in small bowl; mix well. Add to apricots and reserved liquid; mix well. Let stand 20 minutes.

Spoon apricot mixture into pastry-lined pie plate.

Roll out remaining pastry; cut in ½″ strips. Interlace strips in crisscross fashion over filling to make lattice top. Trim strips even with pie edge. Turn bottom crust up over ends of strips. Press firmly to seal edge. Flute edge. Brush crust with milk and sprinkle with sugar.

Bake in 350° oven 1 hour or until golden brown and filling is bubbly. Cool on rack. Makes 6 to 8 servings.

EASY MINCEMEAT PIE

Pie tastes like it's made with homemade mincemeat

1 (1 lb. 12 oz.) jar prepared
   mincemeat (3 c.)
1 c. raisins
2 c. cubed, peeled apples
1 c. water

1 tblsp. lemon juice
2 tblsp. flour
½ c. sugar
Pastry for 2-crust 10" pie

Combine mincemeat, raisins, apples, water and lemon juice in saucepan. Combine flour and sugar; stir into mincemeat mixture. Bring mixture to a boil, stirring constantly. Pour into pastry-lined pie plate.

Roll out remaining pastry; cut in ½" strips. Interlace strips in crisscross fashion over filling to make lattice top. Trim strips even with pie edge. Turn bottom crust up over ends of strips. Press firmly to seal edge. Flute edge.

Bake in 350° oven 55 minutes or until golden brown. Cool on rack. Makes 8 servings.

CRANBERRY RASPBERRY PIE

This outstanding pie was a favorite of our taste-testers

2 c. cranberries, fresh or
   frozen and thawed
1 (10 oz.) pkg. frozen red
   raspberries, thawed
1½ c. sugar
¼ tsp. salt
2 tblsp. quick-cooking
   tapioca

¼ tsp. almond extract
Almond Pastry (recipe
   follows)
1 tblsp. butter or regular
   margarine

Chop or coarsely grind cranberries. Combine with raspberries, sugar, salt, tapioca and almond extract; mix well. Spoon into pastry-lined pie plate. Dot with butter. Roll out remaining dough, cut in ½" strips. Interlace strips in crisscross fashion over filling to make lattice top. Trim strips even with pie edge.

Turn bottom crust up over ends of strips. Press firmly to seal edge. Flute edge.

Bake in 425° oven 10 minutes. Reduce heat to 350° and bake 40 minutes or until golden brown and filling is bubbly. Cool on rack. Makes 6 to 8 servings.

Almond Pastry: Sift together 2¼ c. sifted flour, 1 tsp. salt and 1 tblsp. sugar. Cut in ¾ c. shortening until mixture resembles fine crumbs. Beat together 1 egg yolk, 2 tsp. almond extract and ¼ c. water; sprinkle over flour mixture. Toss with fork to make a soft dough. Divide dough in half; form each half into a ball. Flatten half of dough on lightly floured surface. Roll to about ⅛″ thickness and line 9″ pie plate.

LUSCIOUS CHERRY PIE

In season, use 1 quart fresh pitted red cherries

2 (1 lb.) cans pitted tart red cherries, drained	**2½ tblsp. flour**
	¼ tsp. salt
1¼ c. sugar	**Pastry for 2-crust 9″ pie**

Mix together cherries, sugar, flour and salt. Spoon into pastry-lined pie plate.

Roll out remaining pastry; cut in ½″ strips. Interlace strips in crisscross fashion over filling to make lattice top. Trim strips even with pie edge. Turn bottom crust up over ends of strips. Press firmly to seal edge. Flute edge.

Bake in 450° oven 10 minutes. Reduce heat to 350° and bake 30 minutes or until golden brown and filling is bubbly. Cool on rack. Makes 6 to 8 servings.

BLUE RIBBON CHERRY PIE

"My son asked me to enter this . . . he was sure I'd win"

1 (1 lb. 8 oz.) jar cherry pie filling	**½ tsp. grated lemon rind**
	Pastry for 2-crust 8″ pie
¼ c. sugar	**Butter or regular margarine**
1 tblsp. lemon juice	

Combine cherry pie filling, sugar, lemon juice and lemon rind. Pour cherry pie filling into pastry-lined pie plate. Dot with butter. Adjust top crust and flute edge; cut vents.

Bake in 425° oven 10 minutes. Reduce heat to 350° and bake 30 minutes or until golden brown. Cool on rack. Makes 6 to 8 servings.

CHERRY CHEESE PIE

A Kansas girl says that this is her father's favorite pie

1 (8 oz.) pkg. cream cheese
1 (3 oz.) pkg. cream cheese
½ c. sugar
½ tsp. vanilla
2 egg whites, stiffly beaten
Graham Cracker Crumb Pie
  Shell (recipe follows)

1 (lb.) can pitted tart red
  cherries
Few drops red food color
  (optional)
¼ c. sugar
1 tblsp. cornstarch

Beat cream cheese (11 oz.) until light and fluffy. Blend in ½ c. sugar and vanilla. Fold in beaten egg whites. Spoon into Graham Cracker Crumb Pie Shell.

Bake in 325° oven 25 minutes or until filling is set.

Drain cherries, reserving ½ c. juice. Combine cherry juice, food color, ¼ c. sugar and cornstarch in saucepan. Cook over medium heat until thick. Remove from heat and cool slightly.

Arrange cherries over cheese filling. Spoon sauce over top of cherries. Chill in refrigerator until serving time. Makes 6 to 8 servings.

Graham Cracker Crumb Pie Shell: Combine 1½ c. graham cracker crumbs (about 20), ¼ c. brown sugar, firmly packed, and ⅓ c. melted butter or regular margarine in bowl. Mix until crumbly. Press evenly on bottom and sides of 9″ pie plate.

PINEAPPLE OATMEAL PIE

First-prize winner in a Pennsylvania county fair

3 eggs	⅔ c. quick-cooking rolled
⅔ c. sugar	oats
1 c. brown sugar, firmly	⅔ c. flaked coconut
packed	1 c. raisins
2 tblsp. melted butter or	1 (8¼ oz.) can crushed
regular margarine	pineapple
1 tsp. vanilla	1 unbaked 9″ pie shell

Beat eggs until lemon colored. Gradually add sugars, beating well. Blend in butter and vanilla. Stir in oats, coconut, raisins and undrained pineapple. Pour into pie shell.

Bake in 350° oven 50 minutes or until filling is set. Cool on rack. Makes 6 to 8 servings.

GOOD OLD-FASHIONED PIES

"This tastes like a pie that my great-grandmother used to make," commented a staff taste-tester when she sampled the Old-fashioned Vinegar Pie. The farm wife from South Carolina who submitted the recipe said that it had been in her family for over 100 years. "We think it's different and delicious," she wrote. "It wins every time I enter it in the fair."

A pioneer special from Oklahoma, Heirloom Molasses Pie, is a many-time fair winner. This Oklahoma family likes to serve it with lots of softly whipped cream.

California Chess Pie, rich with eggs, walnuts and raisins has won Blue Ribbons, Sweepstakes and the California State Championship. "I usually stir up several of these pies at a time as they freeze well and they are my family's favorite pie—we raise both the walnuts and raisins on our farm," the winner explained.

OLD-FASHIONED VINEGAR PIE

This recipe is more than 100 years old and still a favorite

½ c. softened butter or
  regular margarine
1¼ c. sugar
2 tblsp. vinegar

3 eggs
1 tsp. vanilla
1 unbaked 8″ pie shell

Cream together butter and sugar until light and fluffy. Add vinegar, eggs and vanilla; beat well. Pour into pie shell.

Bake in 350° oven 45 minutes or until knife blade inserted halfway between center and edge of pie comes out clean. Cool on rack. Makes 6 to 8 servings.

HEIRLOOM MOLASSES PIE

If you wish, you can substitute walnuts for the pecans

4 eggs, separated
1 c. sugar
½ c. light molasses
½ c. light corn syrup
1 tblsp. flour

2 c. milk
¼ tsp. ground cinnamon
2 unbaked 9″ pie shells
1½ c. chopped pecans

Beat egg yolks in bowl. Gradually add sugar, molasses, corn syrup and flour; beat well. Gradually add milk and cinnamon; blending well.

Beat egg whites until stiff peaks form. Gradually blend egg whites into molasses mixture at low speed. Pour evenly into 2 pie shells. Sprinkle with pecans.

Bake in 350° oven 50 minutes or until filling is firm. Cool on rack. Served topped with whipped cream, if you wish. Makes 12 to 16 servings.

CALIFORNIA CHESS PIE

This rich pie will appeal to those with a "sweet tooth"

½ c. butter or regular
  margarine
¾ c. sugar
¼ tsp. salt
3 eggs

¾ c. chopped walnuts
¾ c. chopped seedless
  raisins
1 tsp. vanilla
1 unbaked 9″ pie shell

Cream together butter, sugar and salt until light and fluffy. Add eggs, one at a time, beating well after each addition. Stir in walnuts, raisins and vanilla. Spread mixture in pie shell.

Bake in 425° oven 10 minutes. Reduce temperature to 325° and bake 30 minutes or until filling is set. Cool on rack. Makes 6 to 8 servings.

GOLDEN LEMON CHESS PIE

Smooth, tangy lemon pie is so easy to prepare

2 c. sugar
1 tblsp. flour
1 tblsp. cornmeal
4 eggs
¼ c. milk

¼ c. melted butter or
  regular margarine
¼ c. lemon juice
2 tblsp. grated lemon rind
1 unbaked 9″ pie shell

Combine sugar, flour and cornmeal in bowl. Add eggs, milk, butter, lemon juice and lemon rind. Beat with rotary beater until smooth and well blended. Pour mixture into pie shell.

Bake in 350° oven 40 minutes or until golden brown. Cool on rack. Makes 6 to 8 servings.

ENGLISH WALNUT PIE

This yummy pie has been baked for years by this winner

3 eggs
¼ tsp. salt
⅓ c. sugar
1½ c. light corn syrup

1 tsp. vanilla
1½ c. chopped walnuts
1 unbaked 9″ pie shell

Combine eggs, salt and sugar in bowl; beat well. Add corn syrup and vanilla; beat thoroughly. Stir in walnuts. Pour into pie shell.

Bake in 400° oven 10 minutes. Reduce heat to 350° and bake 35 minutes more or until filling is set. Cool on rack. Makes 6 to 8 servings.

TRADITIONAL THANKSGIVING PUMPKIN AND PECAN PIES

Crisp cold air, crunchy leaves underfoot—it's time to start thinking about how many are coming for Thanksgiving and what pies to serve.

For a change from the basic pumpkin, why not make either our luscious Brown Sugar Pumpkin from Montana, or the Pumpkin Apple Pie from Texas? Or Pumpkin Meringue Pie from Wisconsin with its subtly spiced flavor and high brown-tipped meringue! All have won Blue Ribbons at a fair.

Along with a creamy pumpkin pie, present a pecan pie— either Basic Pecan Pie from Oklahoma, rich, dark and very good, or First-prize Pecan Pie with a crunchy top of chopped pecans, a Blue Ribbon winner from Ohio.

You don't have to wait for Thanksgiving! Any one of these pies would be the perfect finale to a baked bean supper.

BROWN SUGAR PUMPKIN PIE

Spoon a puff of sweetened whipped cream on each serving

1½ c. canned or cooked pumpkin	1 tsp. ground nutmeg
1 c. brown sugar, firmly packed	½ tsp. ground allspice
	3 eggs, beaten
	1 c. evaporated milk
1 tsp. ground cinnamon	1 unbaked 9" pie shell

Combine pumpkin, brown sugar, cinnamon, nutmeg and allspice. Add eggs; mix well. Gradually add evaporated milk; blend thoroughly. Pour into pie shell.

Bake in 425° oven 15 minutes. Reduce heat to 350° and bake 35 to 45 minutes or until knife inserted in center comes out clean. Cool on rack. Makes 6 to 8 servings.

PUMPKIN APPLE PIE

Two pie favorites in one . . . try this treat soon

⅓ c. brown sugar, firmly
   packed

1 tblsp. cornstarch

½ tsp. ground cinnamon

¼ tsp. salt

⅓ c. water

2 tblsp. butter or regular
   margarine

3 c. thinly sliced, peeled
   apples

1 egg, beaten

⅓ c. sugar

¾ c. canned pumpkin

½ tsp. ground cinnamon

¼ tsp. salt

¼ tsp. ground ginger

⅛ tsp. ground cloves

¾ c. evaporated milk

1 unbaked 9″ pie shell

Combine brown sugar, cornstarch, ½ tsp. cinnamon and ¼ tsp. salt in saucepan. Stir in water and butter. Cook over medium heat, stirring constantly, until mixture boils. Add apples; cook over medium heat 4 minutes.

Combine egg, sugar, pumpkin, ½ tsp. cinnamon, ¼ tsp. salt, ginger, cloves and evaporated milk in bowl; mix well.

Pour apple mixture into pie shell. Carefully spoon pumpkin mixture over apples in an even layer.

Bake in 425° oven 10 minutes. Reduce heat to 375° and bake 40 minutes or until filling is set around edge. Cool on rack. Makes 6 to 8 servings.

PUMPKIN MERINGUE PIE

A Wisconsin woman has served this pie for over 40 years

1½ c. canned pumpkin

½ c. sugar

1 tsp. ground cinnamon

½ tsp. salt

¼ tsp. ground nutmeg

¼ tsp. ground cloves

3 eggs, separated

1 c. evaporated milk

1 unbaked 9″ pie shell

⅛ tsp. salt

6 tblsp. sugar

Combine pumpkin, ½ c. sugar, cinnamon, ½ tsp. salt, nutmeg and cloves; mix well. Stir in egg yolks. Gradually blend in evaporated milk. Pour mixture into pie shell.

Bake in 400° oven 35 minutes or until knife inserted halfway between edge and center comes out clean.

Beat egg whites and ⅛ tsp. salt until foamy. Add 6 tblsp. sugar, 1 tsp. at a time, beating well after each addition. Continue beating until stiff peaks form when you lift beater. Spoon meringue over pie filling, spreading evenly to edge of crust to seal all around.

Bake in 425° oven 5 minutes or until meringue is lightly browned. Cool on rack. Makes 6 to 8 servings.

BASIC PECAN PIE

Pie is especially good topped with butter pecan ice cream

1 tblsp. butter or regular margarine	1 tsp. vanilla
	1 c. chopped pecans
1 c. sugar	1 unbaked 9″ pie shell
3 eggs	1 c. pecan halves
1 c. dark corn syrup	

Cream together butter and sugar. Add eggs, one at a time, beating well after each addition. Add corn syrup and vanilla; beat well. Stir in chopped pecans. Pour mixture into pie shell. Arrange pecan halves on top.

Bake in 350° oven 45 minutes or until filling is set. Cool on rack. Makes 6 to 8 servings.

FIRST-PRIZE PECAN PIE

Create an interesting design on top of pie with pecans

3 eggs	½ c. melted butter or regular margarine
½ c. dark corn syrup	
½ c. light corn syrup	½ c. chopped pecans
½ c. sugar	1 unbaked 9″ pie shell
½ tsp. vanilla	½ c. pecan halves

Combine eggs, corn syrups, sugar, vanilla and butter in bowl; beat thoroughly. Stir in chopped pecans. Pour mixture into pie shell. Arrange pecan halves on top.

Bake in 375° oven 40 minutes or until filling is set. Cool on rack. Makes 6 to 8 servings.

BUTTERNUT SQUASH PIE

Whirl drained, cooked squash in blender . . . no lumps

2 lbs. butternut squash, cooked, drained and mashed (1¾ c.)	¼ tsp. ground ginger
	2 eggs, slightly beaten
	1 tblsp. melted butter or regular margarine
1 c. sugar	
½ tsp. salt	1½ c. milk
½ tsp. ground cinnamon	1 unbaked 9″ pie shell
¼ tsp. ground nutmeg	

Combine squash, sugar, salt, cinnamon, nutmeg, ginger, eggs and butter; mix well. Gradually blend in milk. Pour mixture into pie shell.

Bake in 425° oven 45 minutes or until knife inserted halfway between edge and center comes out clean. Cool on rack. Makes 6 to 8 servings.

CREAM AND CUSTARD PIES, SMOOTH AS VELVET

Rich and creamy, smooth as silk is how we would describe these pies. Old-fashioned Butterscotch with its deep delicious flavor is a top favorite at family gatherings, a Wisconsin Blue Ribbon winner informed us—"We think it tastes like penuche candy in a pie shell," she said.

From Colorado comes one of the best coconut cream pies we have ever tested in our Test Kitchens—laced with coconut, it's velvety as can be. We agreed with the judges that it deserved the Purple Ribbon.

A Blue Ribbon Oklahoma winner's entry was Creamy Custard

Pie with a silky texture. "I always dust the bottom unbaked crust with finely crushed cracker meal before I pour in the custard filling—prevents a soggy crust," she said.

OLD-FASHIONED BUTTERSCOTCH PIE

Garnish each wedge with a toasted pecan half if you like

½ c. butter or regular margarine	1 c. milk
1¼ c. brown sugar, firmly packed	4 egg yolks, slightly beaten
1½ c. boiling water	1½ tsp. vanilla
4 tblsp. cornstarch	1 baked 9″ pie shell
3 tblsp. flour	1 c. heavy cream
¾ tsp. salt	½ tsp. vanilla
	1 tblsp. sugar

Brown butter in heavy saucepan over low heat. Stir in brown sugar and boiling water. Bring to a boil; boil 2 minutes, stirring constantly.

Combine cornstarch, flour and salt. Gradually stir in milk; mix until smooth. Stir into brown sugar mixture. Cook, stirring constantly, until mixture comes to a boil and thickens, about 5 to 7 minutes.

Stir a little of the hot mixture into egg yolks; blend well. Gradually stir all of egg yolk mixture into cooked custard; blend well. Cook 1 minute, stirring constantly. Remove from heat. Stir in 1½ tsp. vanilla. Cool well.

Pour filling into pie shell and chill.

Whip heavy cream with ½ tsp. vanilla and sugar until soft peaks form. Serve pie topped with whipped cream. Makes 6 to 8 servings.

COCONUT CREAM PIE

Treat your family to this creamy coconut pie

¼ c. cornstarch	1 tsp. vanilla
⅔ c. sugar	¾ c. flaked coconut
½ tsp. salt	1 baked 9″ pie shell
3 c. milk	6 tblsp. sugar
3 eggs, separated	¼ c. flaked coconut

Combine cornstarch, ⅔ c. sugar and salt in top of double boiler. Gradually add milk, stirring until mixture is smooth. Cook over simmering water, stirring constantly, until mixture is thick enough to mound slightly when dropped from a spoon. Cover and cook 10 minutes, stirring occasionally.

Beat egg yolks. Stir a little hot mixture into egg yolks; blend well. Gradually stir all of egg yolk mixture into cooked custard; blend well. Cook 2 minutes, stirring constantly. Remove from water. Stir in vanilla and ¾ c. coconut. Cool well. Spoon into pie shell.

Beat egg whites until foamy. Add 6 tblsp. sugar, 1 tsp. at a time, beating well after each addition. Continue beating until stiff peaks form when you lift beater. Spoon meringue over pie filling, spreading evenly to edge of crust to seal all around. Sprinkle with ¼ c. coconut.

Bake in 425° oven 5 minutes or until meringue is lightly browned. Makes 6 to 8 servings.

CREAMY CUSTARD PIE

Protein-nutritious custard filling is smooth and delicious

4 eggs, slightly beaten	1 tsp. vanilla
¼ tsp. salt	1 unbaked 9″ pie shell
½ c. sugar	Ground nutmeg
3 c. milk, scalded	

Mix together eggs, salt and sugar. Slowly stir in milk and vanilla. Pour into pie shell. Sprinkle with nutmeg.

Bake in 450° oven 10 minutes. Reduce heat to 325° and bake 30 to 40 minutes or until knife inserted halfway between center and edge of pie comes out clean. Cool on rack. Refrigerate if stored overnight. Makes 6 to 8 servings.

BASIC CUSTARD PIE

Delicate and velvety custard pie that is so easy to make

4 eggs	2½ c. milk, scalded
¾ c. sugar	1 unbaked 9″ pie shell
¼ tsp. salt	¼ tsp. ground nutmeg
1 tsp. vanilla	

Beat eggs slightly. Beat in sugar, salt and vanilla. Gradually add milk. Pour into pie shell. Sprinkle with nutmeg.

Bake in 450° oven 20 minutes. Reduce heat to 350° and bake 15 minutes or until knife inserted halfway between center and edge of pie comes out clean. Cool on rack. Refrigerate if stored overnight. Makes 6 to 8 servings.

SPECIAL-OCCASION PIES

Planning to give a party? Looking for an extraordinary pie to serve with coffee?

Here are two pies that you can fix ahead and refrigerate that will really rate with your guests. Heavenly Chocolate Angel Pie is a three-layer beauty with a light chocolate top, creamy white center and deep rich chocolate base layered into a crunchy pecan meringue crust—wonderful eating! "It's my husband's favorite pie," says the Blue Ribbon winner from Iowa.

Peanut butter fans will be delighted with the cloud-high Peanut Butter Chiffon Pie with its pretzel crumb crust, a Blue Ribbon winner from Wisconsin. "My children are always delighted when I am planning a dinner party for they know that means Peanut Butter Chiffon for dessert."

HEAVENLY CHOCOLATE ANGEL PIE

Elegant chocolate pie that will dazzle your special company

1 (6 oz.) pkg. semi-sweet chocolate pieces	Pecan Meringue Pie Shell (recipe follows)
2 egg yolks	1 c. heavy cream
¼ c. water	½ tsp. vanilla
¼ tsp. ground cinnamon	¼ c. sugar

Melt chocolate pieces in top of double boiler over hot water. Blend in egg yolks and water; stir until smooth. Add cinnamon. Cool slightly.

Spread ½ c. chocolate mixture over bottom of Pecan Meringue Pie Shell. Refrigerate pie and remaining chocolate mixture until it begins to thicken.

Whip heavy cream with ½ tsp. vanilla and sugar until soft peaks form. Spread half of whipped cream over chocolate layer in pie shell.

Fold remaining chocolate mixture into remaining whipped cream. Spread evenly over whipped cream layer in pie shell. Chill at least 4 hours or overnight. Makes 6 to 8 servings.

Pecan Meringue Pie Shell: Combine 2 egg whites, ½ tsp. vinegar, ¼ tsp. ground cinnamon and ¼ tsp. salt; beat until stiff. Gradually add ½ c. sugar and beat until stiff glossy peaks form. Fold in ½ tsp. vanilla and ½ c. chopped pecans. Spread meringue over bottom and sides of well-buttered 9" pie pan. Bake in 325° oven 1 hour or until golden brown. Cool well.

PEANUT BUTTER CHIFFON PIE

Children won't be able to resist their favorite flavor

1 envelope unflavored
   gelatin
¼ c. sugar
¼ tsp. salt
1 c. milk
2 eggs, separated

½ c. creamy peanut butter
¼ c. sugar
1 c. heavy cream, whipped
Pretzel Crumb Pie Shell
   (recipe follows)

Combine gelatin, ¼ c. sugar and salt in saucepan. Gradually add milk and beaten egg yolks; mix well. Cook over medium heat, stirring constantly, until mixture comes to a boil. Reduce heat and cook 5 minutes, stirring constantly. Add peanut butter; stir until blended. Place in bowl of ice water or chill in refrigerator until mixture mounds slightly when dropped from a spoon.

Beat egg whites until foamy. Gradually add ¼ c. sugar, continuing to beat until stiff and glossy. Fold into peanut butter mixture. Fold in whipped cream. Spoon into Pretzel Crumb Pie Shell. Chill 3 hours or until set. Makes 6 to 8 servings.

Pretzel Crumb Pie Shell: Combine ¾ c. pretzel crumbs, 3 tblsp. sugar and 6 tblsp. melted butter or regular margarine; mix well. Press evenly in bottom and sides of 9″ pie plate. Bake in 350° oven 8 minutes. Cool on rack.

LUSCIOUS LEMON PIE

This lovely dessert was chosen as best of 34 pie entries

1 unbaked 9″ graham
   cracker crumb pie shell
1 c. heavy cream
1 (6 oz.) can frozen
   lemonade concentrate,
   thawed

1 (15 oz.) can sweetened
   condensed milk
3 drops yellow food color

Prepare graham cracker crumb pie shell, reserving ⅓ c. crumbs for topping. Chill pie shell.

Whip heavy cream until soft peaks form. Slowly add lemonade concentrate, sweetened condensed milk and food color, mixing well. (Do not overbeat.) Pour into pie shell. Sprinkle with reserved crumbs. Chill at least 2 hours. Makes 6 to 8 servings.

LEMON MERINGUE PIE

Cornstarch keeps this special meringue from weeping

⅓ c. cornstarch	1 tsp. grated lemon rind
1¼ c. sugar	1 baked 9″ pie shell
¼ tsp. salt	1 tblsp. cornstarch
2 c. boiling water	½ c. cold water
3 eggs, separated	2 tblsp. sugar
⅓ c. lemon juice	⅛ tsp. salt
2 tblsp. butter or regular margarine	4 tblsp. sugar

Combine ⅓ c. cornstarch, 1¼ c. sugar and ¼ tsp. salt in 2-qt. saucepan. Gradually stir in 2 c. boiling water. Cook over medium heat, stirring constantly, until thick and clear (about 5 to 7 minutes).

Stir a little hot mixture into egg yolks; blend well. Gradually stir all of egg yolk mixture into cooked custard; blend well. Cook over low heat, stirring constantly, 1 minute. Remove from heat. Stir in lemon juice, butter and lemon rind; stir until butter is melted. Pour into pie shell.

Combine 1 tblsp. cornstarch, ½ c. cold water, 2 tblsp. sugar and ⅛ tsp. salt in small saucepan. Cook over medium heat, stirring constantly, until thick and clear. Cool well.

Beat egg whites until stiff peaks form. Gradually add 4 tblsp. sugar, beating well. Slowly add cooled cornstarch mixture, beating until stiff glossy peaks form. Spoon meringue over pie filling, spreading evenly to edge of crust to seal all around.

Bake in 350° oven 12 to 15 minutes or until meringue is lightly browned. Cool on rack. Makes 6 to 8 servings.

INDEX